Issues in
Career Development

a volume in
Issues in Career Development

Series Editors:
John Patrick, *California University of Pennsylvania*
Grafton Eliason, *California University of Pennsylvania*

Issues in
Career Development

edited by

**John Patrick,
Grafton Eliason**
California University of Pennsylvania

and

Donald L. Thompson
Private Practice

INFORMATION AGE
PUBLISHING

Greenwich, Connecticut • www.infoagepub.com

Library of Congress Cataloging-in-Publication Data

Issues in career development / edited by John Patrick ... [et al.].
    p. cm. — (Issues in career development)
  Includes bibliographical references.
  ISBN 1-931576-06-8 (pbk.) — ISBN 1-931576-07-6 (hardcover)
  1. Career development. 2. Vocational guidance. I. Patrick, John,
1955-
II. Series.
  HF5381.I73 2005
  650.1—dc22
                                                    2005020177

Copyright © 2005 IAP–Information Age Publishing, Inc.

Printed in the United States of America

CONTENTS

INTRODUCTION

The primary purpose of *Issues in Career Development* is to provide a broad look at the field of career development including career counseling, career guidance, career education, and general career development programming, and to examine some of the field's major themes, approaches, and assumptions. We will examine both knowledge from the past as well as what the future might bring. We will bring together a variety of experts/authors from the area of interest and try to provide readers with a framework for action based on the best available research information.

The concept of career development is in a period of dramatic transition resulting from equally dramatic changes in the labor market and the sociocultural environment. Work has a different meaning today than it had 100, 50, or even 10 years ago. Career is now much more tightly interwoven with life, and lifestyle. In that context, career development can only be understood when viewed as a part of the broader concept of human development. Past research clearly indicates that interventions can and do have a significant impact on a variety of career development areas (e.g., job satisfaction, worker productivity), however, there are significant questions that are yet to be answered, and given the changing career/work landscape, significant questions that are not yet known. Particular areas of interest for the future relate to the changing nature of the labor market, gender and minority group issues, socioeconomic trends, and so forth. Historically, much of the research on career development has assumed that psychological factors play the major role in a person's career choices. However, it is becoming increasingly clear that the environment plays a much bigger role than previously assumed. This book series will examine these and other relevant issues in the years to come.

CHAPTER 1

THEORIES OF CAREER DEVELOPMENT

Core Concepts and Propositions

Erik J. Porfeli, Spencer G. Niles, and Jerry Trusty

A theory of career development includes concepts and propositions. Concepts represent the construction materials of a theory while propositions represent the means of fabricating a structure from the identified and defined materials. The aim of this paper is to identify the fundamental constructs and propositions of Super's life-span, life-space theory, Holland's career interest and personality typology theory, Krumboltz and associates' social learning approach to decision making, and Vondracek and associates' developmental contextual metatheory of career development. The intent of this framework is to encourage continued comparison and synthesis of fundamental ideas across theoretical boundaries.

THEORIES OF CAREER DEVELOPMENT
CORE CONCEPTS AND PROPOSITIONS

Career theories reflect the historical context from which they emerge. Generally, theories emanating from the United States emphasize a psychological orientation that highlights how intraindividual variables influence career development. Career theories emphasizing the contextual influences shaping career development processes are less prevalent. Moreover, some career theories stress the career development process (i.e., they describe how careers unfold over time) and other theories describe important factors contributing to the content of career decision-making. Person *and* context variables as well as process *and* content orientations collectively provide the most complete picture of career development theory and practice. Although no one career development theory achieves this lofty goal, there is much to be gained from examining each theory independently and then considering how each theory enhances our overall understanding of career development processes.

The Framework

We employ a common framework to organize the concepts and propositions of the focal theories. The intent of this structure is to act as an aide for the reader to engage in further synthesis than is directly apparent within the text. As is the case in most literatures, theorists and researchers hailing from different career theories discuss and employ similar concepts and propositions under different conceptual and propositional labels. Whether you are a practitioner, researcher, or student, an important task you face is to identify the similarities and differences across theories in order to distinguish, select, and perhaps even build a model that best suits your current needs and your understanding of the phenomena of interest. The intent of this catalogue of prominent career theories and their structure is to promote this process of exploration.

Introduction

This section includes a brief discussion of the historical context from which each theory emerged, the primary career-related phenomena explained by the theory, and the primary players involved in its development and implementation.

Central Concepts and Propositions: Definitions, Investigations, and Development

All scientifically testable theory involves a set of core concepts (i.e., constructs or variables) that aim to define the phenomena of interest. Concepts are tied together with a series of propositional statements that explain how, and often why, the identified concepts are interrelated. A theoretically derived *model* then is a union of theoretical concepts and propositions.

Employing home building as a metaphor for theory construction, concepts represent the building materials and propositions represent the process of combining the materials to fabricate a home. Materials like bricks, mortar, wood, and nails do not necessarily yield a house, as specific processes must be employed in a particular sequence to yield a structurally sound home. Likewise the act of bricklaying, sawing, and hammering can yield many different outcomes depending on the materials involved. Only when the materials and processes are combined in particular ways and sequences does the possibility of a home become a probable outcome. Theory construction, like home building, represents the act of combining materials and processes in a way that yields a unique model of the phenomena of interest.

Within this section, therefore, the basic concepts and propositions of the focal theory will be defined and discussed as a means of reconstructing and ultimately visualizing its basic structure. Given the dynamic nature of theory and research particularly as it relates to popular theories, this section will also include a discussion of the theory's development in response to empirical investigations that have examined its key concepts and propositions.

LIFE-SPAN, LIFE-SPACE THEORY

Introduction

Donald Super (1957) introduced one of the first comprehensive interdisciplinary theories of vocational development[1] and over the course of approximately 40 years continually refined the overall framework to arrive at a life-span, life-space theory of career development, which serves as a cornerstone of modern career development theory.[2]

Life-span, life-space theory has been characterized as a "differential-developmental-social-phenomenological career theory" and as a "segmental" theory (Super, 1969) involving several subtheories that are more or less aligned with several disciplines including psychology, sociology, and economics. Super was an interdisciplinary theorist within the context of the prevailing social scientific orientation of the middle part of the last century, which was often staunchly disciplinary. His life-span, life-space theory is best understood as an outcome of this orientation.

In identifying the sources of his interdisciplinary theory, Super (1984) named four primary disciplines that shaped his thinking. Differential psychology, particularly work on vocational interests (Strong, 1929, 1931, 1933, 1934), contributed the insight that person-level factors (e.g., interests, aptitudes, and achievement) affected occupational behavior and choice. Developmental psychology suggested that humans develop across life stages (e.g., childhood, adolescence, and adulthood) characterized by certain normative contextual demands/tasks (e.g., home-to-school and school-to-work transitions), and that these tasks interact with person-level characteristics to elicit human change and development (Buehler, 1933). Occupational sociology (Miller & Form, 1951) shaped Super's view of career development by suggesting that social structure (Mills, 1959) affects the opportunities, barriers, and ultimately career choices of individuals. Lastly, personality theory suggested that a person's self-concept becomes more salient and more influential throughout adolescence and early adulthood and is a central factor in determining how "people become what they are, how they change, and how they make decisions" (Super, 1984).

Although some have argued for (Super, 1994) and against (Holland, 1994) theoretical integration within the career literature and interdisciplinary thinking across the social science disciplines, many contemporary leaders in life-span psychology and life-course sociology (e.g., Baltes and Elder respectively) are in favor of such efforts (Shanahan & Porfeli, 2002; Vondracek & Porfeli, 2002b). Life-span, life-space theory may thus be viewed as a product of the twentieth century that is situated at the forefront of twenty-first century trends.

The life-span, life-space theory is a complex, multifaceted, interdisciplinary theory of career development. Identifying and depicting all of the concepts and propositions of this model is a complex task. Super (1994) employed three figures to accomplish the task and yet he acknowledged that these figures do not represent all of what the theory suggests. Given the brevity of this review we will center on the core concepts and propositions that have remained fairly stable since Super's early theoretical statements and are represented in either the *ladder model* of life career stages, the *life career rainbow*, or the *archway of career determinants* (Super, 1994).

First, Super (1990, 1994) casts the *life-span* aspect of human development into stages that are depicted by a ladder, where each stage/wrung is loosely defined by the age of the individual. The five stages of the life-span are growth, exploration, establishment, maintenance, and decline.[3] Although at first blush the model appears to be sequential and associated with age, Super (1984) stated that career development proceeds through a maxi-cycle, akin to advancing life stages associated with age, and mini-cycles that involve recycling through stages and experiencing aspects of maxi-cycle stages yet to come during the transitions from one maxi-cycle state to the next. Therefore, an adolescent and an octogenarian can both experience aspects of all five career stages (Super, 1994). This aspect of the theory appears to be quite similar to and perhaps even influenced by Erikson's (1980) stage model of the life-span, particularly in terms of the nature of the stages and the notion of cycling and recycling.[4] Furthermore, this possibility of recycling through stages may be the result from decreasing stability in the workforce as the serial career pattern becomes more common.

Super (1990) added a second dimension to the model to depict the life-space aspect of the model by identifying the impact of life roles within and across life stages (akin to life course sociological thinking) on career development. A rainbow metaphor portrays the life-span and life-space dimensions and the potential for both longitudinal change and cross-sectional differences. Left to right movement across the life career rainbow represents advancing age and stage development, including birth, growth (0-11 years), exploration (12-18 years), establishment (19-25 years), maintenance (25-65 years), and disengagement (65 years and above). The duration of a life-span defines the length of the rainbow. The colors (i.e., width) of the rainbow represent the six major life roles of homemaker, worker, citizen, leisurite, student, and child. The width of the rainbow represents the life-space and one's capacity to take on multiple roles at any given time. A wider rainbow represents a greater capacity. The width of each color band (i.e., life role) represents the emphasis of a life role relative to the others.

The third organizational feature of the theory is the archway of career determinants (Super, 1990). As the title suggests, the metaphor is a roman arch with two sets of core determinants/factors/constructs representing the base of the two columns. One column represents biological/person-level constructs like needs, values, and intelligence and the other column represents geographical/social-structural factors like the economy, society, the prevailing labor market, school, family and peers). The two columns support higher-order career outcomes, depicted by the arch, like the aforementioned career stages and role self concepts. Super (1994) stated that the arch, like any metaphor, has its limits, and one of the fundamental limits of this metaphor is that it fails to depict the interrelated nature within and between the two columns.

These three pictorial representations of the constructs and propositions of the life-span, life-space model are elaborations on Super's (1957) early assertion that people differ in terms of their career-related interests, abilities, learning, and personality factors and that these differences lead to people choosing, establishing, changing and/or maintaining different careers.

CENTRAL CONCEPTS AND PROPOSITIONS: DEFINITIONS, INVESTIGATIONS, AND DEVELOPMENT

Concepts

Of the three pictorial representations, the archway of career determinants most comprehensively depicts the core concepts of the life-span, life-space theory. Person-level concepts include needs, values, interests, intelligence, aptitudes, achievement, personality, exploration and self-concept. Context-level concepts include the economic, labor market, family, school, and peer contexts. These basic person- and context-level concepts combine in various ways to yield career stages, role self-concepts, and ultimately, a holistic image of the self.

Many person-level concepts identified within the life-span, life-space theory have received little direct conceptual specification from life-span, life-space theorists; rather, concepts like needs, values, and intelligence were adopted from their respective literatures and integrated into a general theoretical framework without a great deal of additional specification. Life-span, life-space theorists and researchers, however, have either created (e.g., career maturity) or significantly modified existing concepts (e.g., exploration) to such an extent as to identify them as life-span, life-space concepts that continue to serve as key variables in career research.

Although not direct progeny of the theory, the person-level concepts *vocational exploration* and self-concept have received a great deal of attention in terms of modifications and specification by life-span, life-space theorists and researchers (Super, Starishevsky, Matlin, & Jordaan, 1963). These two key concepts are linked by a dynamic and developmental position, which suggests that both work in tandem to promote career development and maturity.

Super (1984) characterized exploratory behavior "as the prime method of developing personal and situational concepts" (p. 197). Jordaan (1963), working with Super to further refine the life-span, life-space theory during the 1960s and 1970s, explicated the vocational exploration construct along 10 bipolar dimensions (e.g., intended vs. fortuitous and motor vs. mental) and defined vocational exploration as

> activities, mental or physical, undertaken with more or less conscious purpose or hope of eliciting information about oneself or one's environment, or of verifying or arriving at a basis for a conclusion or hypothesis which will aid one in choosing, preparing for, entertaining, adjusting to, or progressing in an occupation. (p. 59)

Super (1957, 1984, 1990; Super, Savickas, & Super, 1996), Jordaan (1963), Havighurst (1964), and others (Blustein, 1989; Blustein, Prezioso, & Schultheiss, 1995; Flum & Blustein, 2000; Grotevant & Cooper, 1986; Savickas, 1984) have expanded the construct of exploration to denote an ongoing and developmental process that involves exploration of the self in conjunction with an active exploration of the world of work, to arrive at a cohesive and well understood self-concept and ultimately a suitable and satisfying career. Vocational exploration, therefore, is a construct that describes a complex constellation of behaviors and cognitions that can lead to an increasing understanding of the self, the environment and/or the fit between the two.

Turning now to the second critical construct within life-span, life-space theory, Super characterized the self-concept in earlier publications (Super, 1957) as a distinct cognitive concept or image of the self and he referred to it as *the self-concept*. Later, Super (Super, 1963) shifted his thinking away from the self-concept as one image of the self and toward a system of multiple self-concepts. One of the commonly cited definitions of the self-concept that allows for the possibility of a self-concept system is the self-concept as a cognitive "picture of the self in some role, situation, or position, performing some set of functions, or in some web of relationships" (Super, 1963).

Although the definition speaks of one *picture*, this picture is specific to a role or situation. Given that humans adopt many roles and find themselves in a wide array of recurring situations, the definition suggests that humans maintain a system of role-specific self-concepts. Conceptually tying the self-concept to the role system allows for the existence of a system of pictures that are distinct but that also share some qualities. A person can be and often is, for example, a parent and a worker. Research demonstrates that aspects of the self-concept, like values for example, demonstrate some consistency across the parent and worker role (Kohn & Schooler, 1983). An interrelated self-concept system allows for this consistency while also remaining true to the common-sense notion that worker and parental roles represent two distinct sets of demands and expectations and therefore self-perceptions.

Savickas (2002) presented a revised definition of the self-concept within the context of an "updated and expanded" version of life-span, life-space theory by explicitly casting the concept into developmental terms. The origin of the self-concept is presumed to be grounded in the ability to perceive the self as an object. The development of this ability during the period spanning infancy to early childhood leads to a mounting collection of self-perceptions concerning how a person fits within his/her environment (e.g., I am good at math and English). This expanding (in terms of number of self-perceptions and perceived interrelationships) constellation coalesces into more abstract person-within-context *self-descriptions* during the period spanning middle childhood to early adolescence (e.g., I am a good student). During middle adolescence to early adulthood (and probably beyond), the person joins together the increasing collection of generally context-specific self-descriptions into more or less abstract, unified, cohesive, and role-specific self-concepts (e.g., I am a bright and hard working person).

A core proposition of the life-span, life-space theory that is not explicitly listed in Super's various lists of propositions (Salomone, 1996) is that the self-concept and vocational exploration reciprocally affect one another. Vocational exploration can lead to alterations and increasing specification of a self-concept and a self-concept can be employed to direct vocational exploration toward or away from certain vocational pursuits as a means of preserving or altering existing person-level qualities and person and environment transactions. Leading into the next central construct, this dynamic process is conceptually presumed and has been empirically demonstrated (Carns et al., 1995; Carver & Smart, 1985) to promote career maturity.[5]

Once termed *vocational maturity* (Super et al., 1957), career maturity is a clear descendent of life-span, life-space theory that has received a great deal of empirical and theoretical attention through its operationalization in the Career Pattern Study and as a result of the introduction (Crites, 1978) and subsequent revision (Crites & Savickas, 1995) of the Career Maturity Inventory. Defined in two ways (Super et al., 1957), vocational maturity (1) "is indicated by the actual life stage of an individual in relation to his expected life stage (based on his chronological age)" and vocational maturity (2) "focuses on developmental tasks and is represented by the behavior of the individual in handling the developmental tasks with which he is actually coping" (p. 132). The latter definition has become the common characterization of career maturity. As listed below within Super's propositions, career maturity is

> a constellation of physical, psychological, and social characteristics; psychologically, it is both cognitive and affective. It includes the degree of success in coping with the demands of earlier stages and substages of career development, and especially with the most recent.

Career maturity, then, is a metaconstruct within life-span, life-space theory, and is primarily an index[6] of a person's ability to successfully employ his or her competencies and historical catalogue of triumphs and failures that contribute to learning and self-confidence to cope with his/her ever-changing, career-related, person-within-context-bound demands across time (Savickas, 2002). In terms of propositions, a person's historical experience guides present functioning and goal formation. Learning (both in the affective and cognitive sense) associated with this history is associated with a person's ability to cope with and successfully meet present demands. Experience and learning, therefore, appear to be two primary mechanisms driving career maturity and career maturity is cast in terms of a person's *readiness* or preparation to meet age- and developmentally-graded demands within and outside the person. Combining both aspects of the index suggests that a person's maturity and ultimately his/her current functioning is guided by his/her ability to cope with ever-changing aspects of the self and the context, which, in turn is shaped by historical events and tasks and their outcomes with respect to learning, self-confidence, personal insight, aspirations, values, and goals (Super, 1957).

PROPOSITIONS

Reviews centering on the development of life-span, life-space theory reveal that Super has presented several versions of the life-span, life-space theoretical propositions since its introduction during the 1950s and these differences are more or less explicitly tied to research outcomes and more or less consistent with previous theoretical statements. Salomone (1996) found in his comprehensive review of Super's propositions that a core set of propositions have remained fairly stable over Super's 40-year career. For those interested in specifically reviewing the propositions, readers are directed to Super's 1980 and 1990 reviews of the theory, which are the most comprehensive and representative of the various iterations.

Although Super employed the term *propositions,* some of the propositional statements are more aptly termed *assumptions* because they support rather than spring directly from the theory. Propositions (Super, 1990) like the following reflect general assumptions that spring from aspects of life-span psychology, occupational sociology, and life-course sociology during the second half of the twentieth century and are indicative of the theory's "segmental" (Super, 1969) quality.

1. People differ in their abilities, personalities, needs, values, interests, traits, and self-concepts.
2. People are qualified, by virtue of these characteristics, each for a number of occupations.
3. Each occupation requires a characteristic pattern of abilities and personality traits, with tolerance wide enough to allow both some variety of occupations for each individual and some variety of individuals in each occupation.

4. The nature of the career pattern—that is, the occupational level
    attained and the sequence, frequency, and duration of trial and sta-
    ble jobs—is determined by the individual's parental socioeconomic
    level, mental ability, education, skills, personality characteristics
    (needs, values, interests traits, and self-concepts), career maturity,
    and by the opportunities to which he or she is exposed (pp. 206-
    208).

Statement 1, for example, suggests that people differ along various
trait-like dimensions, but Super's theory does not explain how or why
people differ, rather, it starts with this assumption and employs it to construct the theory. The prevailing themes that bind these assumptions is
that work is a central aspect of modern life and that humans are active
entities who employ a unique set of characteristics to pursue personally
defined goals, goals that are generally bound by social forces. These ideas
have been further refined and explicated within the developmental-contextual metatheoretical model of career development (Vondracek, Lerner,
& Schulenberg, 1986), which suggests that work is a critical context within
the human ecology, that humans are active agents constructing their own
development, and that human development proceeds within a unique
constellation of contexts where both humans and their contexts are in a
constant and dynamic relationship.

Other propositions (Super, 1990) are more akin to definitional statements of core constructs, as exemplified by the following:

1. Success in coping with the demands of the environment and of the
    organism in that context at any given life-career stage depends on
    the readiness of the individual to cope with these demands (that is,
    on his/her career maturity). *Career maturity* is a constellation of
    physical, psychological, and social characteristics; psychologically
    it is both cognitive and affective. It includes the degree of success
    in coping with the demands of earlier stages and substages of
    career development, and especially with the most recent.

2. Career maturity is a hypothetical construct. Its operational defini-
    tion is perhaps as difficult to formulate as is that of intelligence,
    but its history is much briefer and its achievements even less defin-
    itive. Contrary to the impressions created by some writers, it does
    not increase monotonically, and it is not a unitary trait. (pp. 206-
    208)

The majority of Super's propositions, however, are more akin to propositions based on constructs and relationships springing from life-span,
life-space theory. These propositions and the constructs contained therein

have received varying amounts of conceptual and empirical attention but most have stood the test of empirical scrutiny. This review will center on a few of the most critical propositions that spring from the life-span, life-space approach

Super (1990) suggested that career development proceeds in a sequential, stage-like fashion and is generally associated with age. Super (1990) clearly stated that the association between career development and age is not perfect nor is it necessarily linear because, as his theory suggests, age is a highly generalized proxy for the combined effects of experience and biological and cognitive maturation. Experiences within human contexts are in some cases more bound by age-related norms (e.g., the school grade-level) and in other cases less so (e.g., media exposure), hence experience at the person-level can be highly variable with age. Additionally, for any given person, biological and cognitive development do not typically conform to a linear or smooth curvilinear model of change and are often best characterized as spurts of change that take the appearance of a staircase-like form across time. The standard human growth chart, defined by height and weight, is a good example that takes the appearance of a curvilinear form at the population level but is not reflective of person-level growth spurts that may dramatically diverge from the population trend. Given the variability in biological and cognitive maturation and experience at a particular age, the association between career development and age at the population-level will take on a stage-like pattern. The theory suggests, however, that the stages will occur in the same sequence for all people, while the timing and duration of the stages may be highly variable from person to person.

Relying on this developmental model of change, the theory also suggests that the self-concept and vocationally-related factors like interests, preferences, competencies, and experiences are involved in a dynamic relationship across time. A person's self-concept and, by extension, their occupational self-concept become increasing stable across time as the various aspects of the self coalesce through the process of exploration discussed previously. The mechanism underlying this pattern of increasing stability appears to be akin to the mechanism leading to self-observation generalizations with the social learning theory of career decision making (Krumboltz, 1979).

In terms of career decision-making, the theory suggests that one of the primary aims of individuals establishing or maintaining their worker role is to establish and implement a vocational self-concept tied to the worker role (Super, 1957). Exploration contributes to establishing this self-concept and in finding a place for it in the world of work. Exploration contributes to an increasing awareness and subsequent understanding of a person's emerging and developing vocational self-concept and it, in turn, contributes to vocational maturity through the improved ability to cognitively project and eventually physically place the self into occupational roles that are most suitable to his/her "constellation of physical, psychological, and social characteristics" (Super, 1990, p. 198).

One of the broadest propositions within the life-span, life-space theory suggests that career and life satisfaction is defined by the fit between a person's self-concept system and the roles they occupy.[7] The theory suggests that people will prefer and actively pursue roles that afford the opportunity to enact and develop desirable qualities, particularly those that are central to their self-concept. When such roles are believed to be unavailable, the person may go through a process of change that results in greater consistency between the self-concept and existing opportunities to implement the self-concept. This aspect of the theory demonstrates the person-environment fit lineage of the life-span, life-space model and demonstrates that career development is a lifelong transaction between the person and their environment.

This idea is consistent with systems thinking within the social sciences (Ford, 1987), which suggests that the aim of a living system is to maintain consistency between system requirements and available resources as a means of promoting continued development and functioning. When roles supportive of or consistent with the self-concept are not available or apparent, a person may aim to modify or reorganize available roles to suit the implementation of their self-concepts. Alternatively, a person may elect to modify the self-concept system through personality modification or, in extreme circumstances, personality reorganization to reduce the discrepancy between the self-concept and role affordances and barriers. Savickas (1997) employed and expanded Super's (1990) *career adaptability* construct and suggested that the ability to respond to changes across time, space, and development could be a conceptually stronger way of characterizing career maturity.

CAREER INTEREST AND PERSONALITY TYPOLOGY THEORY: THE INTERACTION BETWEEN PERSONAL INTERESTS AND WORK ENVIRONMENTS

Introduction

Practitioners and researchers involved in making the connection between the constructs of occupational exploration, interests, aspirations and choice typically assume or test the assumption that increased exploration will generally result in a more complete understanding of and match between personal needs and desires and occupational opportunities and demands (Holland, 1992). Two critical dimensions of the exploration construct are self-exploration and environmental exploration (Jordaan, 1963). Holland (1997) proposed, developed, and refined a person-environment-fit model of occupational interests and choice that aims to promote these critical aspects of exploration through a theory-based classification system of people and environments. If use and popularity is an indicator of merit, then Holland's model is a stunning achievement that has dominated the field of occupational interests for the last 20 years.

Clearly an offspring of the trait and factor tradition, Holland endeavored to develop a theoretical model that identified and explained the relationships between trait-like person-level interests, context-level demands and expectations, and career choice, satisfaction, and success in a way that avoided complex occupational classification systems and costly machine-scored inventories (Weinrach, 1984). The Self-directed Search (Holland, 1997) has become a widely accepted alternative to computer-scored classification systems like the Strong (Strong, Campbell, & Hansen, 1985), which continues to be popular within the secondary school guidance system and now includes a Holland code as a part of the summary report.

Holland's theory (1997) rests on three primary assumptions. First, a person's occupational interests and, by theoretical extension, their personality (Gottfredson, Jones, & Holland, 1993; Holland, 1958) can be properly and effectively classified into six groups or *types* that are spatially organized into a hexagon (see Figure 1.1). Those types in close physical proximity along the hexagon are considered to be more closely conceptually related to one another than those that are more distant. Second, work environments can be effectively and accurately assessed and subsequently categorized into the same six types by taking the average (or some other measure of central tendency) interest/personality type of the people who are employed in any given work environment. In other words, the occupational context is a reflection of the sum of its membership (i.e., employees working within that occupational context).[8] Third, people and contexts can be effectively matched through this categorization process. Moreover, placing a person with a particular type within a work context whose membership generally reflects the same type will tend to result in more desirable and effective outcomes for the person (e.g., career satisfaction and success) and the work context (i.e., organizational tasks and goals are effectively accomplished by the employee).

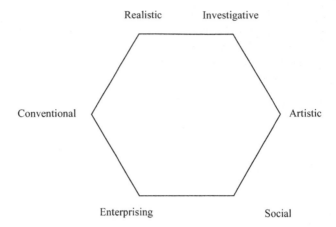

Figure 1.1.   A hexagonal model for defining the psychological resemblance among types and environments and their interactions (Holland, 1997).

CENTRAL CONCEPTS AND PROPOSITIONS: DEFINITIONS, INVESTIGATIONS, AND DEVELOPMENT

Concepts

Holland's theory is primarily focused on the interface between person-level personality types (manifested through interests) and environmental pressures, opportunities, and demands. This brief description identifies two central concepts: personality and interests.

The central concept in Holland's theory is the personality type. Theoretically, interests are presumed to be a direct manifestation of the human personality, therefore personality and interests are presumed to conform to the same general theoretical structure (Gottfredson et al., 1993; Holland, 1958, 1997). Holland (1992), however, does not offer explicit definitions of personality and interests in his primary text but does identify the elements that lead to the development of personality and interests. Abstracting, combining, and paraphrasing several statements from Holland's (1997, pp. 2-3, 7-9, & 17-20) primary text, personality can be characterized as:

A particular, stable, and personal disposition that shapes thinking, perceiving, and action. This disposition is shaped by a catalog of biological predispositions (e.g., heredity) attitudes, behavioral patterns, interests, and competencies that are the result of learning, which occurs at the interface of the person and a "variety of cultural and personal forces including peers, biological heredity, parents, social class, culture, and the physical environment" (p. 2). Parental transmission of genetic potential and parenting thereafter represent significant biological and social forces affecting personality development (i.e., "To some degree, [parental personality] types produce [offspring personality] types"). (p. 17)

Although Holland (1992) described the theory as a "a theory of vocational personalities and work environments" and characterized the theory as a model of "personality types," vocational interests represents a foundational concept supporting the idea that the types are assessed through interests but ultimately reflect personalities. Abstracting, combining, and paraphrasing several statements from Holland's (1992, pp. 2-3, 7-9, & 17-20) primary text, interests can be characterized as:

A preference for certain activities that emerge from experiences that occur at the interface of the person and a "variety of cultural and personal forces including peers, biological heredity, parents, social class, culture, and the physical environment" (p. 2). Parental transmission of genetic potential and parenting thereafter represent significant biological and social forces affecting interest development (i.e., "To some degree, [parental interest] types produce [offspring interest] types"). (p. 17)

Within an encyclopedic text on vocational interests, Savickas (1999) adopted an expanded definition and description of interests that includes statements from Strong (1955):

Interests are the activities for which we have a liking or disliking and which we go toward or away from, or concerning which we at least continue or discontinue the status quo; furthermore, they may or may not be preferred to other interests and they may continue over varying intervals of time. Or an interest may be defined as a liking/disliking state of mind accompanying the doing of an activity, or the thought of performing an activity. (p. 138)

and from Super (1949):

Interests are the product of interaction between inherited aptitudes and endocrine factors, on the one hand, and opportunity and social evaluation on the other. Some of the things a person does well bring him [or her] the satisfaction of mastery or the approval of his [or her] companions, and result in interests. Some of the things his [or her] associates do appeal to him [or her] and, through identification, if he [or she] fits the pattern reasonably well he [or she] remains in it, but if not, he [or she] must seek another identification and develop another self-concept and interest pattern. (p. 406)

Strong's statement explicitly defined the interest concept and Super's statement identified the antecedents and mechanisms that yield interests. Although less detailed, the definition derived from Holland (1997, pp. 2-3, 7-9, & 17-20) touched on both themes by suggesting that interests are preferences for activities that emerge from biological and social origins and experiences.

Holland (1992) indicated that his review of research on vocational interests led to the present personality classification system. Most explicitly connected to the influences that guided or reinforced Holland's typology is a study of interests (Guilford, Christensen, Bond, & Sutton, 1954) conducted on U.S. Air force personnel in which factor analytic techniques yielded the six general interest factors: mechanical, scientific, social welfare, aesthetic expression, clerical and business" (p. 28).[9] These factors are analogous to Holland's realistic, investigative, artistic, social, enterprising, and conventional personality types, and as Holland (1992, p. 6) stated, he was "impressed and reassured" by these findings.

As indicated earlier, the theory suggests that interests are a manifestation of the personality, and therefore, interest assessment tools are also a means of personality assessment (Gottfredson et al., 1993; Holland, 1958, 1959, 1992, 1997). While the theory includes a discussion of the convergence between personality and interest types, the primary text on the theory (Holland, 1992) does not include an explicit statement concerning how they diverge. In terms of empirical support, interests and personality dimensions are weak to moderately associated with one another when the operational definition of personality includes dimensions like extraversion and openness and excludes psychopathogical dimensions, like neuroticism (Osipow & Fitzgerald, 1996). To date, the largest and most recent metaanalysis (Larson, Rottinghaus, & Borgen, 2002) conducted to examine the association between the Holland types and other measures of personality (NEO-PI (FFI), NEO-PI-R, NEO-PI, and NEO) statistically demonstrated that the "glass is half full" (p. 230) and "the glass is half empty" (p. 233) concerning the conceptual link between interests and personality. The results indicate that Holland's types and conceptually similar personality dimensions (e.g., Holland: Social and NEO: Openness) on average share about 4% of their statistical variance.

The bulk of statistical findings suggests a conceptual link between interests and personality (i.e., the glass is half full), but it also suggests that the link is small (i.e., the glass is half empty) thus challenging the position that interest inventories are, in fact, personality inventories. Other researchers (Borgen, 1986; Osipow & Fitzgerald, 1996) have concluded that the issue is ultimately a matter of how interests and personality are defined and an aim of the present review of theoretical concepts and propositions is to promote further consideration of these and other theoretical similarities and distinctions.

The six interest/personality types are realistic, investigative, artistic, social, enterprising, and conventional (Holland, 1985, 1992, 1997). Recall that the six types are conceptually organized into a hexagon, where distance from one type to the next reflects the degree of similarity between types. The types are commonly defined as follows:

Realistic

This type is characterized by a desire to engage in physically demanding activities and those situations that foster the use and design of tools and machines (Holland, 1997). Conversely, this type tends to avoid social-emotionally intense activities and situations. In terms of the distinction between the manipulation of objects or ideas, this type prefers to work with objects. Vocational examples of this type are professional and amateur athlete, farmer, construction worker, and mechanic. Prototypical adjectives of this type are "asocial, materialistic, thrifty, genuine, persistent and uninsightful" (Holland, 1997, p. 19).

Investigative

This type is characterized by a desire and ability to engage in systematic, academic, observational, and scientific pursuits. Although physical and social interactions are a part of most abstract and scientific pursuits, the investigative type tends to prefer the manipulation of ideas and the symbolic representations of reality rather than objects or people. This type tends to avoid activities that require assertive social exchanges aimed at personal extrinsic gain (e.g., human motivation, persuasion, and leadership tasks). Vocational examples are mathematician, professor (particularly scientific disciplines), engineer, and medical technologist

Artistic

This type is characterized by a desire and ability to engage in creative, novel, and innovative activities. Alternatively, this type tends to shy away from objective activities, like those that have a specific direction purpose or behavioral code and suppresses novelty and creativity as in the case of conventional pursuits. Vocational examples are painter, sculptor, musician, philosopher, and interior decorator.

Social

This type is characterized by a desire and ability to engage with, assist, and otherwise manipulate people rather than objects or ideas for emotional (i.e., emotional) gain. This type tends to avoid physically demanding activities and those situations that demand use of and manipulation of tools, machinery, and objects. Vocational examples are social worker, teacher, minister/rabbi/priest or other religious worker, and counselor.

Enterprising

This type is characterized by a desire and ability to engage in leadership, social persuasion other assertive socially intense activities that are aimed at personal extrinsic (i.e., tangible) gain. Alternatively, this type tends to avoid activities that require restraint, analysis, and the manipulation of ideas. Vocational examples are chief executive officer, sales person, administrative assistant, and lawyer.

Conventional

This type is characterized by a desire and ability to navigate within, organize, and maintain a prescribed, well established and codified plan. Alternatively, this type tends to shy away from subjective activities, like those that have little direction purpose or behavioral code and demands creativity and originality as in the case of artistic pursuits. Vocational examples are accountant, timekeeper, postal employee, tax clerk/ employee, and data processor.

Most, if not all, people are believed to exhibit aspects of all six types. People are distinguished from one another by the relative emphasis they place on the six types. Although two people may identify the social domain as the most central aspect of their personality, it is unlikely that they will share the same relative emphasis across all six interest domains. Likewise, work contexts may share the same emphasis among people involved in counseling services, where the social domain tends to be predominant. What distinguishes different jobs within this occupational class is the relative priority structure of the six types. In general, the three most salient types, commonly referred to as the Holland code, are employed to classify people and environments. A Holland code of SAI indicates that the person or context's orientation is toward social, artistic, and investigative pursuits in that order of importance. In the following section, several propositional terms will be introduced that clarify and codify how personality and environmental types are assessed, distinguished, and matched.

PROPOSITIONS

Although often classified as concepts, using the definitions of concepts and propositions discussed at the beginning of this article, the hexagon arrangement of types and terms like consistency, differentiation, congruence and calculus (all discussed below) are more akin to labels for propositional statements that link theoretical concepts (e.g., interests and personality) and that describe the link between subconcepts (e.g., the association between the social and artistic types).

Holland, Whitney, Cole, and Richards (1969) first presented the now well-established hexagonal arrangement of interest/personality types (see Figure 1.1). This spatial arrangement represents a fundamental proposition, a *calculus*. Succinctly stated, the degree of conceptual similarity between the six types is negatively associated with spatial distance. Those types adjacent to one another (e.g., social and enterprising or realistic and investigative) are presumed to be the most conceptually similar. In contrast, those types opposite one another (e.g., realistic and social or investigative and enterprising) are presumed to be the least similar. Holland (1997) employed the term calculus to characterize this spatial arrangement. Contemporary empirical studies generally confirm this spatial arrangement (Prediger, 2000) across major U.S. racial/ethnic groups (Day & Rounds, 1998; Day, Rounds, & Swaney, 1998) but some refute the structural model (Tinsley, 2000) and still others suggest alternative spatial arrangements, like a sphere (Tracey & Rounds, 1996).

Two classes of propositions flow from this superordinate proposition and can be characterized as those focusing on within person or context types and those focusing on the association between person and context types. The first class centers on the distinction between consistency and differentiation, which is employed to describe the relationship between and the relative prioritization of the six personality types at the level of the person and the context.

Consistency involves an indication of the degree of conceptual similarity between a person's or a context's dominant types. Recall that a fundamental assumption of the model is that the six personality types are not independent of one another and that their interrelationships conform to the hexagon structure. Extending from this assumption, the model predicts that people and contexts will tend to exhibit consistency in their orientations. The theory suggests, for example, that people and contexts exhibiting a dominant social (S) orientation (E) and/or the artistic (A) orientations (e.g., SEA or SAE). Conversely, people and contexts exhibiting a dominant social (S) orientation are less likely to also exhibit a dominant realistic (R) orientation (e.g., SR_).The former pattern is classified as being more consistent than the latter.

Supporting the spatial hexagonal arrangement of the types and the idea of consistency, Holland (1997) asserted that discrepant (i.e., low congruence) interest/personality patterns (e.g., equally social and realistic or artistic and conventional) are much less prevalent in people and contexts than are consistent patterns (e.g., social and artistic or realistic and conventional). Therefore, people exhibiting discrepant interests will presumably have more difficulty finding contexts where all of their dominant interests can be employed. Likewise, work environments seeking people with a wide range of interests will have difficulty finding good candidates to fulfill their needs. The infrequent occurrence of discrepant types suggests the notion that people and social groups maintain some measure of internal consistency in interest and personality domains and the hexagon construct reflects this tendency.

Differentiation involves the degree to which a person's interests and a context's opportunities, barriers, and demands form a distinct (as opposed to a diffuse) pattern. A highly differentiated pattern is characterized by a relatively exclusive preference for one or two primary interest/personality types while an undifferentiated pattern is characterized by an equivalent preference for all six interest types (of course the level of preference can range from a consistently weak to a consistently strong orientation toward all six types). According to Holland (1997), people exhibiting a highly differentiated type profile tend to be more "predictable" (p. 33) and have a clearer sense of what they want from the world of work than those exhibiting an undifferentiated pattern. Likewise, highly differentiated contexts, as opposed to highly undifferentiated environments, "encourage a narrow range of behaviors, beliefs, competencies, and interests" (Holland, 1997, p. 50). Holland suggested a developmental perspective to explain how a person's interests become more or less differentiated.

Holland (1997) argued that as individuals move from childhood into adolescence and adulthood, they define their interests by focusing on certain skills and interests and by turning away from others. This process is driven by transactions between the person and their contexts. Holland (1997) asserted that occupational exploration is a fundamental aspect of career development and that it involves the process of identifying personal interests and skills and matching them with occupational characteristics and, ultimately, jobs that demand and reward them. The model suggests that the development of occupational interests and personality through exploration is a critical aspect of the process of moving from an undifferentiated sense of the world of work toward an occupational choice. Moreover, the model suggests a reciprocal effect across time, where interests guide exploration and continued exploration and learning serve to differentiate and crystallize a person's occupational interests. The theory, therefore, predicts that people will tend to exhibit an increasingly differentiated vocational interest and personality pattern as they move from childhood through adulthood (Holland, 1997). Generally, the empirical findings focusing on the differentiation concept are mixed. Holland (1997) cited longitudinal research that supports (e.g., Alvi, Khan,

& Kirkwood, 1990; Taylor, Kelso, Longthorp, & Pattison, 1980) and refutes (e.g., O'Neil, 1977) his assertions concerning differentiation.

The second class of propositions centers on the metaconcept of a person joining, leaving, and living within contexts (i.e., person environment fit). *Congruence* is an indication of the relationship between personal interests and environmental opportunities and barriers. Recall that a principal means of classifying the environment is through an assessment of the central tendency of the interest/personality type of the context's inhabitants. Congruence, then, is to a large extent an indicator of the similarity in activity preferences (and, by extension, personality orientation) of a person and a context's constituency.[10]

Combining aspects of the two classes of concepts, Holland's theory suggests that people who exhibit highly differentiated and consistent configurations of two or three types will (a) typically have a clear vision of their occupational preferences and skills, (b) will be more likely to find an occupation that will support and reward this orientation and, on finding a job with a commensurate orientation, will be (c) more likely to perform up to expectations and to be satisfied with their work experiences. Conversely, people who exhibit a poorly differentiated and inconsistent configuration of interests will be more likely to have the opposite experience. Turning to an example, people who exhibit a highly differentiated orientation toward social pursuits are more likely to gravitate toward and thrive within groups and environments that not only offer many opportunities to engage in socially-oriented activities, like helping others, but also do not offer and perhaps actively suppress realistic activities, like operating machinery. Conversely, the theory also suggests that these highly focused, socially oriented people are more likely to decline in and exit environments and social groups that demand realistic activities and actively suppress a social orientation.

A SOCIAL LEARNING APPROACH TO DECISION MAKING

Introduction

Krumboltz, Mitchell, and Gelatt (1976), Mitchell and Krumboltz (1984, 1996) and Krumboltz (1994, 1996) proposed and subsequently refined a social learning theory of career selection. In their view, the social learning theory of career decision making is an outgrowth of the general social learning of behavior, proposed by Albert Bandura, with its roots in reinforcement theory and classical behaviorism.

It assumes that the individual personalities and behavioral repertoires that persons possess arise primarily from their unique learning experiences rather than from innate developmental or psychic processes. These learning experiences consist of contact with and cognitive analysis of positively and negatively reinforcing events. (Mitchell & Krumboltz, 1984, p. 235)

Such an approach does not imply that humans are

passive organisms that are controlled by environmental conditioning events. Social learning theory recognizes that humans are intelligent, problem-solving individuals who strive at all times to understand the reinforcement that surrounds them and who in turn control their environments to suit their own purposes and needs. (p. 236)

CENTRAL CONCEPTS AND PROPOSITIONS: DEFINITIONS, INVESTIGATIONS, AND DEVELOPMENT

Concepts

Krumboltz and associates have indicated that "real life is always more complicated than our theories" but that it is possible to call attention to the events most influential in determining career selections. In this regard, it is believed that "People learn their preferences by interacting with their environment in a long and complex series of experiences" (Krumboltz, 1994, p. 17). In particular, they point to the following four categories of influence:

1.   Genetic endowment and special abilities. Genetic endowments are inherited qualities such as sex, race, and physical appearance. Special abilities such as intelligence, athletic ability, musical and artistic talents result from the interaction of genetic factors and exposure to selected environmental events.

2.   Environmental conditions and events Factors in this category are generally outside of our control and can involve a wide variety of cultural, social, political, and economics forces. For example, government-sponsored job training programs, such as the Comprehensive Employment Training Act and the Job Training Partnership Act, can provide opportunities for learning new skills and increasing employability. Technological developments (e.g., computer technologies) create new job opportunities and make others obsolete. Legislation related to welfare, labor laws, and union policies influences job availability and facilitates or restricts job entry. Natural disasters can dramatically influence career

opportunities and career paths. Family traditions, as well as neighborhood and community resources, can also significantly affect individuals' career decision making. Job entry requirements can persuade or deter us from considering specific occupational opportunities. Our geographical location can also play a prominent feature in influencing our career choices and the availability of job opportunities (e.g., climatic differences between Maine and Florida result in differences in the availability of some job opportunities, the availability of counseling jobs is greater in the United States than in other countries where counseling concerns are resolved by spiritual leaders).

3. Learning experiences such as *instrumental learning experiences* (ILEs), in which antecedents, covert and overt behavioral responses and consequences are present. Skills necessary for career planning and other occupational and educational performances are learned through successive ILEs. *Associative learning experiences* in which the learner pairs a previously neutral situation with some emotionally positive or negative reaction (observational learning and classical conditioning are examples.)

4. Task approach skills generally include the individual's work habits, mental set, emotional responses, cognitive processes, and problem-solving skills. Task approach skills influence outcomes and are themselves outcomes.

These four types of influence and their interactions lead to several types of outcomes. The outcomes of these learning experiences are not automatic and they are interpreted by individuals differently. Such learning and related observations ultimately become part of the beliefs that individuals develop about themselves, their choices, and the world around them. Although the total number of potential combinations among the concepts discussed above is quite large and any one of these configurations can influence people differently, Social learning theory of career decision making identifies four general ways in which they can influence our career decision making.

These are classified as:

1. *Self-observation generalizations*: overt or covert statements evaluating one's own actual or vicarious performance in relation to learned standards

2. *Task approach skills* (TASs): cognitive and performance abilities and emotional predispositions for coping with the environment, interpreting it in relation to self-observation generalizations, and mak-

ing covert or overt predictions about future events. With relation to career decision making specifically, TASs might include such skills as value-clarifying, goal-setting, alternative-generating, information-seeking, estimating, planning.

3. Actions: entry behaviors that indicate overt steps in career progression (such as applying for a specific job or training opportunity, changing a college major)

The model proposed by Krumboltz and associates underscores the instrumentality of learning experiences as the mechanism that leads to personal preferences for activities as well as task approach skills. Krumboltz, Mitchell, and Gelatt (1976) state,

> It is the sequential cumulative effects of numerous learning experiences affected by various environmental circumstances and the individual's cognitive and emotional reactions to these learning experiences and circumstances that cause a person to make decisions to enroll in a certain educational program or become employed in a particular occupation. (p. 75)

Within a decision theory frame of reference, then, this model suggests that becoming a particular kind of worker or student is not a simple function of preference or choice but "is influenced by complex environmental (e.g., economic) factors, many of which are beyond the control of any single individual" (p. 75). These factors can be learned by the individual, and career decision-making skills can be systematically acquired

PROPOSITIONS

Mitchell and Krumboltz (1984, 1996) have discussed a comprehensive inventory of empirical studies over the past 2 decades that provide considerable evidence to support the processes of the social learning theory of career decision making. It is apparent that the systematic research work of Krumboltz and colleagues has provided significant evidence to support many of the hypotheses that can be generated by the theory and has also provided insight into possible career counseling interventions.

In 1994, Krumboltz identified the testable propositions that derive from the theory as it has evolved. Included are the following:

People will prefer an occupation if

*   They have succeeded at tasks they believe are like tasks performed by members of that occupation

- They have observed a valued model being reinforced for activities like those performed by members of that occupation
- A valued friend or relative stressed its advantages to them and/or they observed positive words and images being associated with it
- A converse set of propositions can be stated as follows:
- People will tend to avoid an occupation if
- They have failed at tasks they believe are similar to tasks performed by people in that occupation
- They have observed a valued model being punished or ignored for performing activities like those performed by members of that occupation
- valued friend or relative stressed its disadvantages to them and/or they have observed negative words and images being associated with it (p. 19).

Among the many practical applications of Krumboltz's (1993) work is that which deals with the private rules of decision making and how these can be influenced by irrational beliefs. For example, Krumboltz has identified several types of problems that can arise from faulty self-observation, generalizations, or inaccurate interpretation of environmental conditions. The problems he identifies include the following:

1. Persons may fail to recognize that a remediable problem exists.
2. Persons may fail to exert the effort needed to make a decision or solve a problem.
3. Persons may eliminate a potentially satisfying alternative for inappropriate reasons.
4. Persons may choose poor alternatives for inappropriate reasons.
5. Persons may suffer anguish and anxiety over perceived inability to achieve goals.

Accordingly, Krumboltz suggests that beliefs can cause distress in career decision making when they are rooted in faulty generalizations, a self-comparison with a single standard, exaggerated estimates of the emotional impact of an outcome, false causal relationships, an ignorance of relevant facts, and an overemphasis on low-probability events. Krumboltz contends that some of these beliefs and private rules in career decision making are related to the fact that making decisions is a painful process that involves at least four causes of stress: threat to self-esteem, surprise, deadlines, and absence of allocated time for decision making. These stresses, in turn, lead to such reactions as impaired attention, increased cognitive rigidity, narrowed perspectives, and displaced blame.

Finally, Krumboltz contends that there are methods for identifying and acting on the faulty private beliefs and related stresses identified in the counseling process. They include: assessment of the content of the client's self-observation and world view generalizations and the processes by which they arose; structured interviews; thought listing; *in vivo* self-monitoring; imagery; career decision-making simulations; reconstruction of prior events; behavioral inferences and feedback; use of psychometric instruments; use of cognitive restructuring techniques to help alter dysfunctional or inaccurate beliefs and generalizations; use of simple positive reinforcement; providing appropriate role models; use of films including problem-solving tasks for viewers; use of computerized guidance systems to provide and reinforce problem-solving tasks; teaching belief-testing processes; analyzing task-approach skills and teaching those in deficit (Krumboltz, 1993; Krumboltz & Henderson, 2002; Mitchell & Krumboltz, 1984, 1996); the use of the Career Beliefs Inventory (Krumboltz, 1994) to identify presuppositions that may block people from achieving their career goals.

The comprehensive conceptualizations by Krumboltz and colleagues about decision making and those proposed interventions leading from these conceptualizations have made extensive contributions to the professional literature. In contrast to many other theories, which either tend to emphasize environmental factors, particularly social and economic influences on decision making, at the expense of intrapsychic individual processing of psychological events or vice versa, the social learning approach, as articulated by Krumboltz, has attempted to take a more holistic approach by providing insight into each of these sets of factors and their interactions.

For these reasons and others, the social learning theory of Krumboltz is seen as having considerable compatibility with major aspects of Super's self-concept theory and with the development of interests as depicted by Holland's hexagon (Krumboltz, 1994). Indeed, some (Krumboltz & Henderson, 2002) have suggested that the learning principles that form the basis for the social learning theory may be fundamental to processes embedded within other career development theories and may provide an accounting of the mechanisms that underlie other theories.

DEVELOPMENTAL CONTEXTUAL METATHEORY
OF CAREER DEVELOPMENT

Introduction

Drawing from Bronfenbrenner's (1979) ecological model of human development, the application of developmental contextualism to career development asserts that contexts, like members of a family or elements in a system, are linked to one another and hierarchically arranged (Vondracek et al., 1986). Linkages may or may not be readily apparent or intentional and the effect of a linkage may be direct and/or indirect. Rather than consider the school, the family, and the neighborhood contexts as distinct, developmental contextualism urges the researcher to view all of these contexts as embedded within and defined by the host community and the person as an occupant of a constellation of differing but interconnected contexts. One important distinguishing feature of a community is the nature and strength of the linkages between subcontexts and the extent to which these connections benefit their citizens. A popular example of context linkage in the vocational literature is research and discussion on the transition from school to full-time work (Grant, 1988; Hamilton & Hamilton, 1999; Reitzle, Vondracek, & Silbereisen, 1998; Stern, Finkelstein, Stone, Latting, & Dornsife, 1994).

Developmental contextual theory (DCT) is derived from contextualism and organicism (Vondracek et al., 1986). The contextualism position asserts that individual-level development and differences are primarily a product of the environment, while organicism takes the position that the person's development is determined by his/her biological nature and inheritance and that human development proceeds along a trajectory that can be promoted or hindered, but not fundamentally transformed, by the context. DCT represents aspects of both to arrive at a complex concept of the person embedded within an array of contexts.

DCT, respecting aspects of both positions, suggests that the person is a complex multilevel system which engages in, moves between, and is "embedded" within multiple contexts (Vondracek & Fouad, 1994). Vondracek and his colleagues (Vondracek & Kawasaki, 1995; Vondracek & Porfeli, 2002a) have suggested that researchers and practitioners who employ theoretical models that account for interacting and linked contexts and that take a systems approach to person-level functioning (e.g., Ford, 1987; von Bertalanffy, 1968) are likely to advance the field (Vondracek & Porfeli, 2002a).

Developmental contextualism is a metatheoretical perspective; therefore, the perspective can be used as a starting point from which to evaluate and modify person-level theories that do not include strong theoretical connections to more macro or context-level factors like economic trends, educational policy, labor laws and the sociocultural context. Conversely, the perspective can be employed to evaluate and modify context-level theories that do not include strong theoretical connections to more micro or person-level factors like interests, personality, and self-concepts. Combining these two possibilities, developmental contextualism can be employed as an overarching model bridging several theoretical perspectives to arrive at a view of the person and context as being in constant dynamic interaction. Its primary use is as a lens through which to examine and develop content-specific theories or as a bridge linking, for example, traditionally person-centered psychological theories and context-centered sociological theories of human development (Vondracek & Porfeli, 2002b).

While the approach is rich in mechanisms leading to the notion that the person is inextricably linked to the context, DCT does not forward an extensive catalogue of concepts that characterize domains of human life (e.g., career development). Rather than offer a set of content-specific concepts, DCT offers a way to approach the task of defining these terms. DCT can aid researchers and theorists interested in evaluating fundamental constructs that hail from organismic or contextualistic theoretical traditions and redefine them in ways that are consistent with the idea that people and contexts are inextricably linked.

CENTRAL CONCEPTS AND PROPOSITIONS: DEFINITIONS, INVESTIGATIONS, AND DEVELOPMENT

Concepts

The essential concepts within DCT are the *person* and the *context*. Although most theories within social science could be characterized in this way, defining these two constructs and their interrelationships is the focus of DCT. DCT presents both concepts in a way that demonstrates the complex, constantly changing, dynamic relationships between the two. This representation of the person as embedded within an array of contexts leads to a new and useful way of interpreting and designing career development research and practice.

The Person

Deriving a definition from DCT and life-span psychology, Vondracek, Lerner, and Schulenberg (1986) view the person as an entity that is constantly changing and developing in response to internal and environmental experiences. In contrast to an extreme version of organicism that conceives of human functioning and development as an outcome of exclusively person-level (e.g., biological and psychological) processes and a radical version of contextualim that points to contextual (e.g., social structure) features as the prime mover of development, developmental-contextualism asserts that human functioning and development is the result of the transaction between biological/physical, psychological, and social processes that occur within and outside the person. Therefore, humans shape their contexts, contexts shape their inhabitants, and human change and development occur at the interface of the person and the context. This leads Vondracek, Lerner, and Schulenberg (1986) to conclude that "the individual is a producer of his/her own development" (p. 74). This view of the person deserves further explanation. First, humans exist and operate on multiple levels. These levels can be defined by their physical/biological, psychological, or social characteristics. Many aspects of human functioning and behavior can be categorized as being a mixture of all three categories.

Second, all levels from the intracellular human system to the cosmos are inextricably linked along biological/physical, psychological, chronological, and social dimensions.[11] The person and the context are conceptually, then, as Gollin states (as cited in Vondracek et al., 1986) "one life process."

Third, the human lifespan demonstrates some measure of consistency and variability in terms of current functioning (within and between age groups) and some measure of stability and plasticity in terms of change and development (within and between age groups) across all people (Lerner, 1984; Lerner et al., 1996).

The Context

The context, in simple terms, is that which exists outside of the organism. Vondracek, Lerner, and Schulenberg's (1986) application of developmental contextualism in the career development domain utilized Bronfenbrenner's (1979) ecology of human development as a basis for defining the context of career development. Accordingly, they describe it as a complex array of nested, career-related contextual structures (Bronfenbrenner, 1979) defined by their inhabitants, their physical and social characteristics, and the degree to which the interaction between the two yields systematic career-related opportunities and barriers (i.e., affordances) for each inhabitant. These nested structures are the product of the dynamic interaction between present-day human and nonhuman influences and preexisting physical (Stokols, 1978, 1982, 1995) and social structures (Vondracek et al., 1986).

Bronfenbrenner's (1979) theory of human ecology starts from the frame of reference of the person and employs mainly social factors to characterize the human context as being composed of nested (i.e., hierarchically arranged) social structures. Vondracek, Lerner, and Schulenberg (1986) employed Bronfenbrenner's (1979) classification system as a means of organizing the complex hierarchical array of career-related human contexts across the life-span, although they noted that other models, such as Gibson's (1979) model of affordances could also serve this purpose. The following section contains a list of the concepts describing the various types/levels of the human ecology and brief definitions and examples of each.

The Microsystem

Defined as "a pattern of activities, roles, and interpersonal relations experienced by the developing person in a given setting with particular physical and material characteristics" (Bronfenbrenner, 1979, p. 22). Examples of a microsystem include the family, the classroom, or the work group within a larger organization.

The Mesosystem

Defined as "a set of interrelationships between two or more settings in which the developing person becomes an active participant" (Bronfenbrenner, 1979, p. 209). In general, the mesosytem acts as a more or less apparent bridge between microsystems. Examples of mesosystems can include contexts that bridge two microsystems (e.g., Parent-teacher associations or vocational education programs that link the classroom to the work setting). Mesosystems can be, and typically are, the result of concurrent participation in distinct but related contexts, like the impact felt while attempting to be an active and successful participant in both the work and family settings.

The Exosystem

Defined as "consisting of one or more settings that do not involve the developing person as an active participant but in which events occur that affect, or are affected by what happens in that setting" (Bronfenbrenner, 1979, p. 237). Examples of exosystems are the school board, the city council, and the community. For example, the city council may dictate community zoning changes that transform residential property into a new airport. The airport will have an impact on the community members. This impact will vary along many dimensions including the proximity of a person's residence to the facility and their travel habits. In summary, the council has little direct impact on any one person (the council does not go door to door enforcing legislation); rather, the council guides an array of meso and microsystems within the community, which in turn, tend to have a direct impact on the person. Recall, however, that the frame of reference is the person; therefore, the city council is a microsystem for a select group within the community, namely those people who preside on the city council.

The Macrosystem

Defined as "the consistency observed within a given culture or subculture in the form and content of its constituent micro, meso, and exosystems, as well as any belief system or ideology underlying such consistencies" (Bronfenbrenner, 1979, p. 258). Examples of a macrosystem are the compulsory educational system, the government, and the cultural context that binds exosystems together.

Bronfenbrenner's (1979) ecological classification system can be used to identify and examine the relationships between the person and their contexts and within and between distinct levels of the context (e.g., relationships within a parent's microsystem: work and family or between the micro and macrosystems: family and the neighborhood). From the ecological system definitions above, the reader should note that the distinctions made between the different system levels are less dependent on the size of a particular context (both in terms of physical and social dimensions) and are more dependent on the person's relationship to the context. As in the city council example above, one person's microsystem can be another person's exosystem.

Figure 1.2 contains a model of career development (Vondracek et al., 1986, p. 79) and text describing the various elements of the model (Niles, Trusty, Vondracek, & Porfeli, 2002, p. 9), including the various levels of context that influence a person's career development across the life-span. While Bronfenbrenner's model emphasizes the impact of human contexts on humans and their development, the heart of the DCT lies in the dynamic exchange between the person and his/her microcontexts. For example, the family shapes the child, but the child also shapes the family. Although a child may contribute to shaping the mother's work environment through the additional demands the child places on her, the more immediate and powerful effect is on the family microsystem. Combining this idea with the notion of nested contexts suggests that a person can have an influence on larger contextual systems through his/her impact on more proximal contexts. Figure 1.2 can therefore be employed to infer not only the potential impact of a person on a context, but also guide the estimation of the impact of a person on varying levels of the context.

In summary, the person is defined in part by the context and the context is defined in part by the person. People select, delete, and modify their contexts to achieve their goals and, in turn, human contexts select, delete, and modify their inhabitants to achieve their goals (e.g., mission statements). DCT asserts that humans select and affect their contexts and their contexts select and affect them; therefore, both humans and human contexts can be cast as the outcome of a complex dynamic process and humans are both products of and producers of their own development.

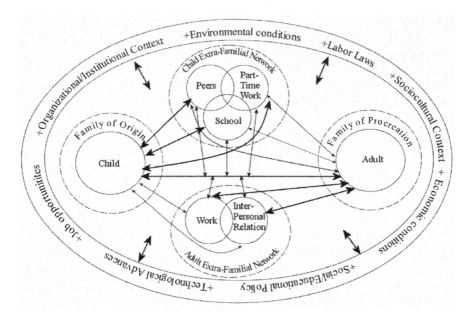

Child: This circle represents the developing child embedded in multiple contexts like the family (permeable (dashed) circle), peers, and school and it represents the child as a self-constructing living system. Take notice of the bolded and fainter arrows connecting the child to the child's extra-familial network, the adult, and the adult's extra-familial network respectively. The bolder arrows represent relationships that are presumed to be stronger than the fainter arrows.

The child extra-familial network: This permeable context includes aspects like school, peers, part-time work, and other community affiliations like church and community service organizations. The overlapping circles in the model suggests that the sub-contexts have shared and independent aspects as in the case of a child who has friends that do and do not attend the same school as sh/e. The arrow connecting this context to the developing person suggests that these contextual factors affect the magnitude and direction of the developing child and they affect the relationship between the child and the child as an adult.

The developing person: The arrow connecting the child and adulthood circle represents the child moving through adolescence and into adulthood.

Adult: This circle represents the child as an adult embedded within a network of family, romantic, and adult-as-parent relationships.

The adult extra-familial network: This context represents the adult social context outside of the home. When the child becomes an adult, they enter and become members of this context. The child's parental figures are also members of this context. The arrows connecting aspects of this context to the developing person suggests that these contextual factors affect the magnitude and direction of the developing child and they affect the relationship between the child and the child as an adult.

All of the aforementioned contexts are embedded within and affected by larger community and societal-level factors like the sociocultural context, governmental policy, and current economic conditions and trends (Niles, Trusty, Vondracek, & Porfeli, 2002, p. 9).

Figure 1.2.   A developmental-contextual model of vocational development across the lifespan (Niles et al., 2002).

PROPOSITIONS

The essential propositions within DCT center on the nature of human development. This definition of human development is rooted in the idea that the person and the environment are elements of a single, albeit complex, entity that involves a host of causal mechanisms and interactions that lead to developmental variability and constancy. The developmental-contextual metamodel is at its heart a unique conception of how humans change and develop. DCT distinguishes between human development and change by suggesting that development is a specific type of change. Human development is characterized as change that is systemic, organized, and successive; change that takes on an identifiable developmental form and sequence and generally moves the organism from a less differentiated to a more differentiated state (Vondracek et al., 1986).

DCT asserts that human development occurs at the juncture of the person and the context. Person-level functioning and social contexts affect current and future person- and context-level functioning as well as developmental pathways and their trajectories (Vondracek et al., 1986). DCT suggests a host of mechanisms that culminate in the idea that people shape contexts and contexts shape people; therefore, people and contexts are inextricably linked. Therefore, a group of people in a particular time and place can become a context and a constellation of contexts can define significant aspects of a person. For example, if a judge, a prosecutor, a public defender, a bailiff, and a court reporter occupy a room, we are more likely to perceive the context as a court proceeding than as a classroom. Likewise, if a person has attended law school, has spent a great deal of time in a courtroom, and has not yet resided in a prison, then we are more than likely to characterize the person as a lawyer.

As humans move across time and space, their history, current structure and functioning, and goals change in response to experiences that occur within and outside the person. In terms of history, a person's goals and experiences today becomes tomorrow's history and the fodder for new goals and experiences. Conversely, human contexts bear the direct (e.g., changing social conventions or physical structures) and indirect (e.g., pollution from neighboring contexts) weight of human influence, they change in terms of their history, current structure and function, and goals (e.g., mission statements). Given that history, current structure and functioning, and goals are in constant flux at both the person and context-level and the person and their contexts are linked, human development is probabilistic in nature.

The term *probabilistic epigenesis* is incorporated within the DCT notion of human development to reinforce the idea that the present structural coherence of a human limits the potential for its variability in the next moment to such an extent that a certain range of developmental change is probable (Vondracek, 1990). Change outside this range is not impossible, but it is improbable.[12] Probable development is a more quantifiable way of characterizing what is commonly referred to as *normal* development.

DCT supports the assertion that human development proceeds according to a biological ground plan within a changing context and is most akin to "probabilistic epigenesis" (Vondracek, 1990; Vondracek et al., 1986). Human development is partly epigenetic because the human architecture is bounded by a biological ground plan that shapes the components (e.g., organs) and general structural relationships between the components (e.g., how the organs are arranged and interact). Although humans vary in the physical and psychological development, we demonstrate far more similarities than differences.

Although our genetic ground plan contributes to humans being far more similar than different, differences abound; therefore, development is *probabilistic* because an innumerable set of person- and context-level factors interact to shape developmental trajectories thus yielding individual differences (Lerner, 1991). A critical factor contributing to person-to-person differences is the notion of timing. Given that development proceeds at the interface of the person and the context, *when* a person (in terms of developmental status) and a contextual stimulus (historical time) meet is of central importance (Lerner, Perkins, & Jacobson, 1993). Timing is a central aspect of the probabilistic nature of development. Person-level factors (i.e., maturation) and context-level *pathways* (e.g., the school to work transition) serve to move people within and between particular contexts for varying amounts of time, at varying points during the life-span, and during specific historical eras. As an example, imagine how two adolescents making the transition from school to work in the United States would differ if one did so during peace time and one made the transition during war time. Furthermore, imagine how they would differ if one made the transition to full-time work at the age of 16 years and the other did so at the age of 22 years.

Thinking about career development, late adolescence appears to be a critical point along the life-span. Why? A pure organismic response may assert that career maturity, for example, is a manifestation of cognitive maturation and age is a proxy for cognitive development; therefore late adolescence represents the period during the life-span when a person is capable of taking the necessary steps to find and choose a career. A contextualistic response, on the other hand, may cast career maturity as the byproduct of a societal structure that compels older adolescents to make the transition from school to work; therefore, people develop in response to societal forces that compel people to become a working member of society. The difficulty of combining a psychological model of any complexity with a contextual model is stated within the literature (Shanahan & Porfeli, 2002; Vondracek & Porfeli, 2002b) and becomes apparent when, for example, one considers adding several person-level psychological variables like exploration, interests, personality, and self-concepts to contextual variables like SES and race. Conceivably, contextual factors could have an influence on all psychological variables both individually and in complex configurations of linear and curvilinear relationships. Moreover, contextual variables could affect the relationships (e.g., mediator and moderator effects) between the psychological variables. Clearly DCT can yield a great deal of conceptual and empirical complexity.

This level of complexity and the probabilistic notion of development are supported when thoughtfully designed, extensively tested, and well-executed interventions produce unanticipated beneficial or detrimental person- and group-level outcomes. Thinking in terms of a system (von Bertalanffy, 1968), stimulus directed at one level of analysis affects all other levels of the system either directly or indirectly. Although the impact may be trivial at other, more distal levels, the developmental contextual-perspective challenges the researcher to at least consider collateral effects and associations and to realize that the impact at one level is not as insulated from the other levels as we may hope or believe.

Summary

The theories we have discussed represent the rich scholarly tradition that characterizes the career development field. The theories have points of convergence as well as uniqueness. Each theory was developed in the twentieth century to respond to emerging questions concerning the nature and development of careers across the life-span. Similarly, they each possess strengths and limitations. Generally, career theories in the United States deemphasize contextual influences in career development. Obviously, this is a strength of DCT and, to a lesser degree, of Super's and Krumboltz's theories. Holland's theory provides the best example of a theory that is readily translated into practice. Thus, it is not surprising that Holland's theory has generated the greatest amount of research. In terms of Super's view of life-space, the current interest many people have concerning a balance between life roles (e.g., work and family) reinforces the importance of advancing the life-space discussion. Despite the important contributions within each of the theories, all of the theories need strengthening with regard to describing career development processes and interventions for diverse populations. What seems most clear, however, is that the theories we have discussed offer a broad view of career development that serves as a useful foundation for continued theory construction in the twenty-first century.

NOTES

1. Ginsberg's (1951) work on career choice and Strong's (1930) work on occupational interests represent other significant contributions to the career literature during this time. These examples, however, focused squarely on one concept within the career domain, while Super's contribution seeks to explain the domain of career development.

2. Super has stated in several publications that the life-span, life-space approach is not a theory, however, this approach does fit the parameters of a theory outline in the introduction of this paper.

3. A thorough description of all of the stages is beyond the scope of this paper. The reader is directed to a recent review (Niles & Harris-Bowlsbey, 2002) and update (Savickas, 2002) of life-span, life-space theory for an expanded description of the career stages.

4. Other authors (Sharf, 1992) have identified similarities between Erikson and Super.

5. The empirical link deserves greater attention.

6. Interestingly, Super (1957) proposed (albeit dismissively) that the vocational maturity construct could be mathematically divided by age and thus transformed into a "quotient" (the vocational maturity quotient) akin to intelligence.

7. In terms of conceptual precision, concepts like career and life satisfaction have not received much attention.

8. During the mid to late 1980s, the theory was modified to include the use of supplemental information (e.g., typical job tasks).

9. After Guilford et al. (1954) present their six interest factors they foreshadow aspects of Holland's hexagon by cautiously suggesting a possible association between the clerical, mechanical, and scientific interest factors and between the clerical and business factors.

10. Interestingly, Guilford et al. (1954) foreshadowed the idea of classifying people and environments via interest dimensions, as well as the idea of congruence in the following quote:

The results [in the article] support well the belief in vocational-interest factors as genuine psychological unities. Our social culture (and no doubt this is true of other cultures) has established firmly in the minds of men the vocational stereotypes represented. The degree of precision of the stereotype varies from one factor to another, as the class of occupations and tasks involved represents a more or less coherent or restricted picture. It is also apparent that each stereotype of an occupational or job class bears some consistent relationships to generalized interest factors, and to some extent the vocational factors [mechanical, scientific, social welfare, aesthetic expression, clerical and business] show relationships to one another, as between mechanical and scientific interests and between business and clerical interests.

The structure of the interest domain then, can be conceived as having a large number of basic, generalized dimensions that cut across many vocational lines, superimposed upon which are a few social stereotypes of broad job families whose existence as unities rests upon knowledge of vocations. This knowledge of vocations includes predominantly the awareness of social goals and also combinations of aptitudes needed for these vocations. This knowledge is, of course, generally naïve. One way in which knowledge of aptitudes plays a role may be as follows. A person who possesses in higher-than-average degree combinations of abilities that enable him to surpass in mechanical tasks derives satisfaction in doing those things. He is rewarded and hence by reinforcement an interest develops. (p. 29)

11. As Lewtontin (as cited in Vodracek, Lerner, & Schulenberg, 1986) points out, in theory all levels of analysis are conceptually linked (as in the relationship between intracellular processes and cosmic events), but in practice, in some levels the magnitude of the link is so weak as to be "effectively decoupled."

12. Probable and improbable are used in place of more absolute terms like possible and impossible to include the host of historical examples of people who have exhibited change that was deemed impossible.

REFERENCES

Alvi, S. A., Khan, S. B., & Kirkwood, K. J. (1990). A comparison of various indices of differentiation for Holland's model. *Journal of Vocational Behavior, 36*(2), 147-152.

Blustcin, D. L. (1989). The role of goal instability and career self-efficacy in the career exploration process. *Journal of Vocational Behavior, 35*(2), 194-203.

Blustein, D. L., Prezioso, M. S., & Schultheiss, D. P. (1995). Attachment theory and career development: Current status and future directions. *Counseling Psychologist, 23*(3), 416-432.

Borgen, F. H. (1986). New approaches to the assessment of interests. In S. H. Osipow (Ed.), *Advances in vocational psychology: The assessment of interests.* (Vol. 1, pp. 83-125). Hillsdale, NJ: Erlbaum.

Bronfenbrenner, U. (1979). *The ecology of human development.* Cambridge, MA: Harvard University Press.

Buehler, C. (1933). *The human life course as a psychological subject.* Leipzig, Germany: Hirzel.

Carns, A. W., Carns, M. R., Wooten, H. R., Jones, L., Jones, L., Raffield, P., & Heitkamp, J. (1995). Extracurricular activities: Are they beneficial? *Texas Counseling Association Journal, 23*(2), 37-45.

Carver, D. S., & Smart, D. W. (1985). The effects of a career and self-exploration course for undecided freshmen. *Journal of College Student Personnel, 26*(1), 37-43.

Crites, J. O. (1978). *Career maturity inventory.* Monterey, CA: CTB/McGraw-Hill.

Crites, J. O., & Savickas, M. L. (1995). *Career maturity inventory.* Monterey, CA: CTB/McGraw-Hill.

Day, S. X., & Rounds, J. (1998). Universality of vocational interest structure among racial and ethnic minorities. *American Psychologist, 53*(7), 728-736.

Day, S. X., Rounds, J., & Swaney, K. (1998). The structure of vocational interests for diverse racial-ethnic groups. *Psychological Science, 9*(1), 40-44.

Erikson, E. H. (1980). *Identity and the life cycle.* New York: W. W. Norton & Company.

Flum, H., & Blustein, D. L. (2000). Reinvigorating the study of vocational exploration: A framework for research. *Journal of Vocational Behavior, 56*(3), 380-404.

Ford, D. H. (1987). *Humans as self-constructing living systems: A developmental perspective on behavior and personality.* Hillsdale, NJ: Erlbaum.

Gibson, J. J. (1979). *The ecological approach to visual perception.* Boston: Houghton-Mifflin.

Ginzberg, E. (1951). *Occupational choice.* New York: Columbia University Press.

Gottfredson, G. D., Jones, E. M., & Holland, J. L. (1993). Personality and vocational interests: The relation of Holland's six interest dimensions to five robust dimensions of personality. *Journal of Counseling Psychology, 40*(4), 518-524.

Grant, W. T. (1988). *The forgotten half--non-college youth in America: An interim report on the school-to-work transition.* Washington, DC: William T. Grant Foundation.

Grotevant, H. D., & Cooper, C. R. (1986). Exploration as a predictor of congruence in adolescents' career choices. *Journal of Vocational Behavior, 29*(2), 201-215.

Guilford, J. P., Christensen, P. R., Bond, N. A., Jr., & Sutton, M. A. (1954). A factor analysis study of human interests. *Psychological Monographs, 68*(4), 38.

Hamilton, S. F., & Hamilton, M. A. (1999). Creating new pathways to adulthood by adapting German apprenticeship in the United States. In W. R. Heinz (Ed.), *From education to work: Cross national perspectives* (pp. 194-213). New York: Cambridge University Press.

Havighurst, R. J. (1964). Youth exploration and man emergent. In H. Borow (Ed.), *Man in a world at work* (pp. 215-236). Boston: Houghton-Mifflin.

Holland, J. L. (1958). A personality inventory employing occupational titles. *Journal of Applied Psychology, 42*, 336-342.

Holland, J. L. (1959). A theory of vocational choice. *Journal of Counseling Psychology, 6*, 35-45.

Holland, J. L. (1985). Making vocational choices: A theory of vocational personalities and work environments (2nd ed.). Englewood Cliffs, NJ: Prentice-Hall.

Holland, J. L. (1992). *Making vocational choices: A theory of vocational personalities and work environments* (3rd ed.). Odessa, Fl: Psychological Assessment Resources.

Holland, J. L. (1994). Separate but unequal is better. In R. W. Lent (Ed.), *Convergence in career development theories: Implications for science and practice* (pp. 45-51). Palo Alto, CA: CPP Books.

Holland, J. L. (1997). *Making vocational choices: A theory of vocational personalities and work environments* (3rd ed.). Odessa, FL: Psychological Assessment Resources.

Holland, J. L., Whitney, D. R., Cole, N. S., & Richards, J. M. (1969). An empirical occupational classification derived from a theory of personality and intended for practice and research. *ACT Research Reports, 29*, 22.

Jordaan, J. P. (Ed.). (1963). Exploratory behavior: The formation of self and occupational concepts. In *Career development; self-concept theory: Essays in vocational development* (pp. 42-78). Princeton, NJ: College Entrance Examination Board.

Kohn, M. L., & Schooler, C. (1983). *Work and personality: An inquiry into the impact of social stratification.* Norwood, NJ: Ablex.

Krumboltz, J. D. (Ed.). (1979). A social learning theory of career decision making. In *Social learning and career decision making* (pp. 19-49). Cranston, RI: Carroll Press.

Krumboltz, J. D. (1993). Integrating career and personal counseling. *Career Development Quarterly, 42*, 143-148.

Krumboltz, J. D. (1994). The career beliefs inventory. *Journal of Counseling and Development, 72*, 424-428.

Krumboltz, J. D. (1996). A learning theory of career counseling. In M. Savickas & B. Walsh (Eds.). *Integrating career theory and practice.* Palo Alto, CA: CPP Books.

Krumboltz, J. D., & Henderson, S. (2002). A learning theory for career counselors. In S. Niles (Ed.), *Adult career development: Concepts, issues and practices* (3rd ed., pp. 41-58). Tulsa, OK: National Career Development Association.

Krumboltz, J. D., Mitchell, A., & Gelatt, H. G. (1976). Applications of social learning theory of career selection, *Focus on Guidance, 8*, 1-16.

Larson, L. M., Rottinghaus, P. J., & Borgen, F. H. (2002). Meta-analyses of Big Six interests and Big Five personality factors. *Journal of Vocational Behavior, 61*(2), 217-239.

Lerner, R. M. (1984). *On the nature of human plasticity.* New York: Cambridge University Press.

Lerner, R. M. (1991). Changing organism-context relations as the basic process of development: A developmental contextual perspective. *Developmental Psychology, 27*(1), 27-32.

Lerner, R. M., Lerner, J. V., von Eye, A., Ostrom, C. W., Nitz, K., Talwar-Soni, R., & Tubman, J. G. (1996). Continuity and discontinuity across the transition of early adolescence: A developmental contextual perspective. In J. Brooks-Gunn (Ed.), *Transitions through adolescence: Interpersonal domains and context* (pp. 3-22). Hillsdale, NJ: Erlbaum.

Lerner, R. M., Perkins, D. F., & Jacobson, L. P. (1993). Timing, process, and the diversity of developmental trajectories in human life: A developmental contextual perspective. In D. A. Devenny (Ed.), *Developmental time and timing* (pp. 41-59). Hillsdale, NJ: Erlbaum.

Miller, D. C., & Form, W. H. (1951). *Industrial sociology: The sociology of work organizations* (2nd ed.). New York: Harper & Row.

Mills, C. W. (1959). *The sociological imagination.* New York: Oxford.

Mitchell, L. K., & Krumboltz, J. D. (1984). Social learning approach to career decision making: Krumboltz's theory. In D. Brown, L. Brooks, & Associates. (Eds.), *Career choice and development* (pp. 235-280). San Francisco: Jossey-Bass.

Mitchell, L. K., & Krumboltz, J. D. (1996). Krumboltz's learning theory of career choice counseling. In D. Brown, L. Brooks, and Assoc. (Eds.), *Career choice and development* (3rd ed., pp. 233-276). San Francisco: Jossey-Bass.

Niles, S. G., & Harris-Bowlsbey, J. (2002). *Career development interventions in the 21st century.* Upper Saddle River, NJ: Merrill Prentice Hall.

Niles, S. G., Trusty, J. T., Vondracek, F. W., & Porfeli, E. J. (2002). *Investigating career development from childhood to early adulthood* (Grant Proposal). Philadelphia: Pennsylvania State University, University Park.

O'Neil, J. M. (1977). Holland's theoretical signs of consistency and differentiation and their relationship to academic potential and achievement. *Journal of Vocational Behavior, 11*(2), 166-173.

Osipow, S. H., & Fitzgerald, L. F. (1996). *Theories of career development* (4th ed.). Boston: Allyn & Bacon.

Prediger, D. J. (2000). Holland's hexagon is alive and well—though somewhat out of shape: Response to Tinsley. *Journal of Vocational Behavior, 56*(2), 197-204.

Reitzle, M., Vondracek, F. W., & Silbereisen, R. K. (1998). Timing of school-to-work transitions: A developmental-contextual perspective. *International Journal of Behavioral Development, 22*(1), 7-28.

Salomone, P. R. (1996). Tracing super's theory of vocational development: A 40-year retrospective. *Journal of Career Development, 22*(3), 167-184.

Savickas, M. L. (1984). Career maturity: The construct and its measurement. *Vocational Guidance Quarterly, 32*(4), 222-231.

Savickas, M. L. (1997). Career adaptability: An integrative construct for life-span, life-space theory. *Career Development Quarterly, 45*(3), 247-259.

Savickas, M. L. (1999). The psychology of interests. In A. R. Spokane (Ed.), *Vocational interests: Meaning, measurement, and counseling use* (pp. 19-56). Palo Alto, CA: Davies-Black.

Savickas, M. L. (2002). Career construction: A developmental theory. In D. Brown & Associates (Eds.), *Career choice and development* (4th ed., pp. 149-205). San Francisco: Jossey-Bass.

Shanahan, M. J., & Porfeli, E. J. (2002). Integrating the life course and life-span: Formulating research questions with dual points of entry. *Journal of Vocational Behavior, 61*(3), 398-406.

Sharf, R. S. (1992). *Applying career development theory to counseling.* Belmont, CA: Brooks/Cole.

Stern, D., Finkelstein, N., Stone, J. R., III, Latting, J., & Dornsife, C. (1994). *Research on school-to-work transition programs in the United States* (No. MDS-771). Berkeley, CA: National Center for Research in Vocational Education.

Stokols, D. (1978). Environmental psychology. *Annual Review of Psychology, 29*, 253-295.

Stokols, D. (1982). Environmental psychology: A coming of age. In A. G. Kraut (Ed.), *The G. Stanley Hall lecture series* (Vol. 2, pp. 159-205). Washington, DC: American Psychological Association.

Stokols, D. (1995). The paradox of environmental psychology. *American Psychologist, 50*(10), 821-837.

Strong, E. K., Jr. (1929). Diagnostic value of the vocational interest test. *Educational Record, 10*, 59-68.

Strong, E. K., Jr. (1931). *Change of interests with age.* Oxford, England: Stanford University Press.

Strong, E. K., Jr. (1933). Aptitudes versus attitudes in vocational guidance. *Psychological Bulletin, 30*, 585.

Strong, E. K., Jr. (1934). Permanence of vocational interests. *Journal of Educational Psychology, 25*, 336-344.

Strong, E. K., Jr. (1955). *Vocational interests 18 years after college.* Minneapolis, MN: University of Minnesota Press.

Strong, E. K., Jr., Campbell, D. P., & Hansen, J. (1985). *The Strong-Campbell Interest Inventory.* Minneapolis, MN: National Computer Systems.

Strong, E. K., Jr., & Mackenzie, H. (1930). Permanence of interests of adult men. *Journal of Social Psychology, 1*, 152-159.

Super, D. E. (1949). *Appraising vocational fitness by means of psychological tests.* New York: Harper & Row.

Super, D. E. (1957). *The psychology of careers; an introduction to vocational development.* New York: Harper & Row.

Super, D. E. (1963). Self-concepts in vocational development. In J. P. Jordaan (Ed.), *Career development; Self-concept theory: Essays in vocational development* (pp. 17-32). New York: College Entrance Examination Board.

Super, D. E. (1969). Vocational development theory: Persons, positions, and processes. *The Counseling Psychologist, 1*(1), 2-9.

Super, D. E. (1984). Career and life development. In D. Brown & L. Brooks (Eds.), *Career choice and development: Applying contemporary theories to practice* (pp. 192 - 234). San Francisco: Jossey-Bass.

Super, D. E. (1990). A life-span, life-space approach to career development. In L. Brooks (Ed.), *Career choice and development: Applying contemporary theories to practice* (2nd ed., pp. 197-261). San Francisco: Jossey-Bass.

Super, D. E. (1994). A life-span, life-space perspective on convergence. In R. W. Lent (Ed.), *Convergence in career development theories: Implications for science and practice* (pp. 63-74). Palo Alto, CA: CPP Books.

Super, D. E., Crites, J. O., Hummel, R. C., Moser, H. P., Overstreet, P. L., & Warnath, C. F. (1957). *Vocational development; a framework for research.* New York: Bureau of Publications, Teachers College, Columbia University.

Super, D. E., Savickas, M. L., & Super, C. M. (1996). A life-span, life-space approach to career development. In D. Brown, L. Brooks, & Associates (Eds.), *Career choice and development* (3rd ed., pp. 197-261). San Francisco: Jossey-Bass.

Super, D. E., Starishevsky, R., Matlin, N., & Jordaan, J. P. (1963). *Career development; self-concept theory: Essays in vocational development.* New York: College Entrance Examination Board.

Taylor, K. F., Kelso, G. I., Longthorp, N. E., & Pattison, P. E. (1980). Differentiation as a construct in vocational theory and a diagnostic sign in practice. *Melbourne Psychology Reports, 68*, 1-18.

Tinsley, H. E. A. (2000). The congruence myth: An analysis of the efficacy of the person-environment fit model. *Journal of Vocational Behavior, 56*(2), 147-179.

Tracey, T. J. G., & Rounds, J. (1996). The spherical representation of vocational interests. *Journal of Vocational Behavior, 48*(1), 3-41.

von Bertalanffy, L. (1968). *General system theory.* New York: George Braziller.

Vondracek, F. W. (1990). A developmental-contextual approach to career development research. In W. A. Borgen (Ed.), *Methodological approaches to the study of career* (pp. 37-56). New York: Praeger.

Vondracek, F. W., & Fouad, N. A. (1994). Developmental contextualism: An integrative framework for theory and practice. In R. W. Lent (Ed.), *Convergence in career development theories: Implications for science and practice* (pp. 207-214). Palo Alto, CA: CPP Books.

Vondracek, F. W., & Kawasaki, T. (1995). Toward a comprehensive framework for adult career development theory and intervention. In S. H. Osipow (Ed.), *Handbook of vocational psychology: Theory, research, and practice* (2nd ed., pp. 111-141). Mahwah, NJ: Erlbaum.

Vondracek, F. W., Lerner, R. M., & Schulenberg, J. E. (1986). *Career development: A life-span developmental approach.* Hillsdale, NJ: Erlbaum.

Vondracek, F. W., & Porfeli, E. J. (2002a). Counseling psychologists and schools: Toward a sharper conceptual focus. *Counseling Psychologist, 30*(5), 749-756.

Vondracek, F. W., & Porfeli, E. J. (2002b). Integrating person- and function-centered approaches in career development. *Journal of Vocational Behavior, 61*(3), 386-397.

Weinrach, S. G. (1984). Determinants of vocational choice: Holland's theory. In D. Brown, Brooks, L., Delworth, U., & Hanson G. R. (Ed.), *Career choice and development* (pp. 61-93). San Francisco: Jossey-Bass.

CHAPTER 2

JOHN HOLLAND

An Enduring Legacy

John Patrick, Kelly Tuning, Jessica Grasha, Amy Lucas, and April Perry

This chapter examines the central key concepts of John Holland's typology theory of career development. Applications of his theory are also discussed including vocational assessment, an occupational classification system, as well as future applications of his work germane to career development theory.

John Holland is perhaps one of the most recognized theorists in the field of career development and choice. In his own way, he has tried to answer a rather simple question "How does an individual find, choose, and maintain a career?" As Miller (1998) notes and a cursory review of the literature (Gottfredson, 1999; Herr, 1997; Herr & Cramer, 1996; Niles & Harris-Bowlsbey, 2002; Osipow & Fitzgerald, 1996; Sharf, 2002; Zunker, 2002) confirms, Holland's theory has survived nearly 30 years of empirical scrutiny and remains one of the premier theories in the vocational literature. There is hardly a practicing counselor today who has not encountered his work, and in some way chooses to incorporate aspects of

Issues in Career Development, 43–52
Copyright © 2005 by Information Age Publishing
All rights of reproduction in any form reserved.

his approach into their own practice. In recognition of his enduring legacy this article will describe John Holland's theory, constructs, and practical applications as they relate to career development. A final section will discuss future applications of his work.

JOHN HOLLAND'S TYPOLOGY THEORY

Central to John Holland's theory is that career choice and development is representative of a person's personality, in that people express themselves, their interests and values, through their work choices and experience (Holland, 1992). Individuals are initially attracted to a career by their personalities and other variables such as age, gender, culture, social class, intelligence, and level of education that constitute their personal background (Herr & Cramer, 1996; Holland, 1992; Sharf, 2002; Zunker, 2002). Thus, a comparison of self with one's perception of an occupation becomes a major determinant in the development of career choice.

Holland's theory is best described as structural-interactive "because it provides an explicit link between various personality characteristics and corresponding job titles and because it organizes the massive data about people and jobs" (Weinrach & Srebalus, 1990, p. 40). Holland (1982) suggested his theory was structural interactive in that: (1) the choice of an occupation is an expression of personality and not merely a random event; (2) members of an occupational group have similar personalities and similar histories of personal development; (3) since people in an occupational group have similar personalities, they will respond to many situations and problems in similar ways; and (4) that occupational achievement, stability, and satisfaction depend on congruence between one's personality and the job environment (p. 2). Additionally four assumptions serve as a template for Holland's theory:

1. In our culture, most persons can be categorized as one of six types: realistic, investigative, artistic, social, enterprising, or conventional.

2. There are six kinds of environments: realistic, investigative, artistic, social, enterprising, or conventional.

3. People search for environments that will let them exercise their skills and abilities, express their attitudes and values, and take on agreeable problems and roles.

4. A person's behavior is determined by an interaction between his personality and the characteristics of his environment (Holland, 1973, pp. 2-4).

The key to using Holland's theory (1973, 1992) with career decision makers is in understanding his typology of six personality types and corresponding work environments. Essentially, John Holland sees an individual as a product of both heredity and environment. As a result of this interaction with heredity and the environment, an individual develops preferences for dealing with environmental demands often known as his or her modal personal orientation. In making career choices, the career decision maker is seeking to find a career that satisfies one's preferred modal personal orientation and will make vocational choices accordingly (Zunker, 2002).

Holland's typology categorized people into one of six broad types of personality: realistic (R) in which the person prefers activities that require the explicit, ordered, or systematic, manipulation of objects, tools, machines, and animals and generally avoids educational or therapeutic activities; investigative (I) in which the person primarily enjoys activities that entail the observational, symbolic, systematic, and creative investigation of physical, biological, and cultural phenomena to understand such phenomena and a concomitant aversion to persuasive, social, and repetitive activities; artistic (A) in which the preference is for ambiguous, free, unsystematized activities that entail the manipulation of physical, verbal, or human materials to create art forms or products with a distaste for explicit, systematic, and ordered activities; social (S) in which activities that entail the manipulation of others to inform, train, develop, cure, or enlighten is preferred coupled with an aversion to explicit, ordered, systematic activities involving materials, tools, or machines; enterprising (E) in which activities that entail the manipulation of others to attain organizational or economic gain are preferred to the exclusion of observational, symbolic, and systematic activities; and conventional (C) in which preferred activities entail the explicit, ordered, systematic manipulation of data, such as keeping records, filing materials, reproducing materials, organizing written and numerical data according to a prescribed plan, operating business and data processing machines to attain organizational or economic goals coupled with an aversion to ambiguous, free, exploratory, or unsystematized activities (Holland, 1973, pp. 14-18; as cited in Herr & Cramer, 1996). Holland (1973) also classified work environments using the same six personality types.

More commonly, Holland's typology is commonly referred to as the RIASEC model and is represented figurally by a hexagon showing the relationships within and between personality types (Holland, 1985, 1992). Each personality type is a point on a hexagon. This model positions each personality type to show accurate distances between the relations between each type, as well as how closely they are correlative to each other (also known as calculus in Holland's theory). Those types that are adjacent to each other on the hexagon (realistic, investigative) share the most common of characteristics, and those that are furthest apart share the least in common (artistic, conventional).

Holland (1973, 1985, 1992) has also proposed that personality types can be arranged in a coded system following the RIASEC model and devised to indicate the person's primary and secondary types. These codes are in three-letter combinations with each letter corresponding to one of the six personality types described earlier. For example, a code of SIA would indicate that an individual is very much like an individual in social occupations, and somewhat like those in both investigative and artistic occupations. Work environments have also been classified in similar fashion.

In a recent statement on his theory, Holland (1997) has proposed that psychological types can be characterized in terms of "beliefs." He suggests that each personality type has "a distinctive belief about the self and about the consequences of actions and each model environment promotes different belief systems" (Gottfredson, 1999, p. 19). Further, most persons have a personal career theory (PCT) about careers. An individual's PCT, comprised of beliefs, ideas, assumptions, and knowledge (self and occupational) serves as a guide in making career decisions and explains why one persists in a career (Reardon & Lenz, 1999).

KEY CONSTRUCTS

Crucial to employing the RIASEC model with career decision makers are four key concepts: Congruence, consistency, differentiation, and vocational identity (Holland 1985). Congruence is perhaps the most important construct in Holland's theory. Congruence is the degree of fit between an individual's personality orientation and actual or contemplated work environment. If a person is in a congruent work environment (e.g., an investigative type working as a paleontologist) then he or she will tend to be more satisfied with their career choice and thus perform better. As Niles and Harris-Bowlsbey (2002) note, a primary goal of using Holland's theory in career counseling is "helping clients identify and connect with congruent work environments" (p. 53).

Consistency refers to the degree of relatedness between types. This can best be represented by looking at the first two letters of the three-letter code. Types that are adjacent on the hexagon (e.g., SE) have more in common than types that are opposite (e.g., AC). High consistency is evident when the first two letters of their three letter code are next to each other on the hexagon (SA), medium consistency when the first two letters of the code are separated by a letter on the hexagon (SI), and low consistency when the first two letters of the code are separated by two letters on the hexagon (SR). Though it is not usually a goal of career counseling to make individuals more consistent, it is important to point out that it may be difficult to find a work environment that can incorporate all aspects of their personality. Thus, identifying avocational interests may also become a focus of attention as a means to express those aspects of personality that cannot be incorporated in the work environment.

Differentiation is concerned with the degree to which a person or a work environment is well-defined. Some people appear to strongly resemble one personality type while others appear to be undifferentiated and have interests, competencies, and abilities that fit several personality types. Those who are undifferentiated are likely to have difficulty in making career decisions and are likely to need career interventions that help them to achieve greater differentiation among Holland types (Niles & Harris-Bowlsbey, 2002).

Vocational identity is defined as the "possession of a clear and stable picture of one's goals, interests, and talent" (Holland, 1985, p. 5). How well-defined are career goals? To what extent are career goals made with sufficient occupational and self-information? A person with many goals would be considered to have low vocational identity.

PRACTICAL APPLICATIONS

Gottfredson (1999) has noted the many practical contributions John Holland's theory has had for career counselors and career decision makers. Chief among these contributions have been the development of vocational instrumentation and the Holland Occupational Classification system.

Vocational Assessment

Congruence, differentiation, consistency, and vocational identity are the key constructs used when applying Holland's theory to career counseling practice. Assessment instruments developed by John Holland and his associates are most often used to appraise these constructs with the results providing career counseling content for the career decision maker (Niles & Harris-Bowlsbey, 2002). The inventories most commonly employed for this purpose include The Self-Directed Search (SDS) (Holland, Fritzsche, & Powell, 1994)), the Vocational Preference Inventory (VPI) (Holland, 1985), and My Vocational Situation (MVS) (Holland, Gottfredson, & Power, 1980) and "are all designed to provide vocational assistance cheaply and with minimal counselor intervention" (Gottfredson, 1999, p. 21).

The inventory that has gained world wide acceptance when applying Holland's theory to practice is the SDS. The SDS is a self-administered, self-scored, and self-interpreted vocational inventory designed to transform a person's particular activities, competencies, and self-estimates into their Holland three-letter code (Brown, 2001). Further, the SDS serves as a basis for relating self-assessment to appropriate occupations. The SDS consists of an assessment booklet (used to find a test taker's three-letter SDS summary code), an occupations finder (listing of occupations classified according to their three-letter Holland summary code), and an interpretive guide titled "You and Your Career." This guide provides additional information, activities, and readings related to using Holland's theory in career decision-making (Niles & Harris-Bowlsbey, 2002). The inventory is available in different versions based on reading level, setting, and language spoken. Additionally, the SDS is available via the Internet. The SDS is also useful in exploring the concepts of congruence, consistency, and differentiation as it relates to career readiness.

Individuals tend to more satisfied and make a better adjustment when they are in a work environment or occupation that is congruent with their personality type (Spokane, 1985). Reardon and Lenz (1999) note that congruence between expressed and assessed interest measures as measured by the SDS is most useful in assessing a client's readiness to move forward in the career decision-making process. They note that if the code of the first ideal (or daydream) occupation noted on the SDS or their current vocational aspiration is closely related to their SDS summary code, this may indicate "that the client is thinking in a stable, systematic way about his or her interests and possibilities" (p. 107). Additionally, this aspiration appears to be maintained over time (Holland, Powell, & Fritzsche, 1994).

Differentiation refers to the distinctness of a personality or work environment. A career decision maker who resembles one Holland personality type and much less resemblance to the other RIASEC types is considered to be highly differentiated whereas a person who resembles all personality types equally is undifferentiated. Reardon and Lenz (1999) note that a highly differentiated SDS summary code can be more reliably used than an undifferentiated code and is useful in assisting clients to see "why making a career choice might be difficult when everything or nothing seems of interest" (p. 110). Career decision makers who have an undifferentiated profile may benefit from being exposed to all six basic types of work environments and based on these experiences develop a new Holland summary code based on personal experience (Weinrach & Srebalus, 1990).

Consistency is measured by examining the relationship between the first two letters of the SDS summary code. If the SDS summary code is consistent in terms of the RIASEC model then this is "considered a positive sign and typically correlates with more stability in work history and direction of career choice" (Reardon & Lenz, 1999, p. 109). Typically when an SDS summary code lacks consistency, it becomes important to explore those dimensions of their personalities that may not be able to be expressed in work and to identify educational, leisure, and other avocational interests that may allow for their expression.

The identity scale of the MVS is often used to explore the construct of vocational identity with career decision makers. The MVS is a simple hand-scored, self-administered form that is most often used as a screening device for looking for people who need intensive career counseling because of poor vocational identity (Lunneborg & Westbrook, 1985). A high vocational identity scale score on the MVS indicates confidence and a general ability to make good career decisions, whereas a low vocational identity score suggests that these career decision makers may have career interests that are unstable and may not be able to adequately use self and occupational knowledge gained from completing the SDS (Reardon & Lenz, 1999).

The utility of the three letter Holland code can be seen in other vocational assessment devices. Interest inventories, aside from the SDS and VPI, which provide Holland summary codes include the Career Assessment Inventory, Kuder General Interest Survey, and Strong Interest Inventory (Kapes & Whitfield, 2001).

Occupational Classification System

An outgrowth of Holland's typology theory has been the classification of occupations according to the psychological characteristics of its workers. Six general classes of occupations have been identified: realistic occupations (includes skilled trades and many technical and some service occupations), investigative occupations (includes scientific and some technical occupations), artistic occupations (includes artistic, musical, and literary occupations), social occupations (includes educational and human service occupations), enterprising occupations (includes managerial and sales occupations), and conventional occupations (includes office and clerical occupations, Herr & Cramer, 1996, p. 157). Each general class of occupations has subclasses and are further arranged by the years of education required. To date over 12, 800 occupations have been arranged and each has been assigned a three letter Holland summary code (Gottfredson & Holland, 1989).

Weinrach and Srebalus (1990) have noted that this classification system has been used for organizing occupational information, analyzing work histories, and developing occupational exploration plans for clients. Filing occupational information according to the Holland occupational classification scheme provides easy access to occupational information based on the results of the SDS and other test results that produce a Holland summary code. Workers who are contemplating a job change can, through an analysis of their work histories, be shown similarities among various jobs and make more effective career choices as a result. Occupational exploration can be facilitated by having career decision makers examine occupations based on the similarity with their SDS summary code.

The Holland Classification taxonomy has generally withstood empirical scrutiny and has been applied to a variety of interest measurement and career planning aids (Herr & Cramer, 1996). Most notably the Holland system has been incorporated in the Department of Labor's O*NET system, used with the DISCOVER microcomputer guidance system, and in a variety of career education activities and printed materials within the schools (American College Testing Program, n.d.; U.S. Department of Labor, n.d.).

FUTURE APPLICATIONS

Gottfredson (1999) in summarizing John Holland's collective work posits that "the usefulness of Holland's theory and typology are so well accepted that they are now assumed as background—the context within which much career practice and career research is conducted" (p. 24). Against this backdrop, Gottfredson has suggested four areas where research on Holland's theory may be useful: (1) development and socialization, (2) personal and environmental change, (3) assessment of environments and environmental influences, and (4) effects of vocational interventions delivered by alternate means and media. He suggests that further consideration on the development of personality dispositions as they relate to occupational entry, achievement, and/or attainment may be useful. How do people cope with incongruent environments? What modes of coping and under what circumstances do people leave incongruent environments or seek to change the work environment? How can researchers directly measure the work environment using diverse samples of occupations rather than employing approximate methods especially as it applies to congruence? Perhaps most importantly, additional work is needed to develop technologies for constructing, understanding, and selecting appropriate career interventions with career decision makers (Gottfredson, 1999).

CONCLUSION

John Holland's theory has transformed the way career counseling is rendered today. His theory is among the most widely used and has stimulated extensive research. His theory has probably had the greatest impact through the vocational assessment inventories that have been developed, most notably SDS, and the Holland Classification System which has been used with numerous career planning aids and publications (Yost & Corbishley, 1987). Perhaps one of his most enduring legacies is that future developments in vocational psychology will most often lie on the theoretical and practical foundations set by John Holland (Gottfredson, 1999).

REFERENCES

American College Testing Program. (n.d.). *World of work map: Underlying research*. Retrieved February 21, 2003, from http://www.act.org/wwm/research.html

Brown, M. B. (2001). Review of the Self-Directed Search (4th ed.). In B. S. Plake & J. C. Impara (Eds.), *14th mental measurements yearbook*. Lincoln, NE: University of Nebraska Press. Retrieved February 20, 2003 from the WEBSPIRS database.

Gottfredson, G. D. (1999). John L. Holland's contributions to vocational psychology: A review and evaluation. *Journal of Vocational Behavior, 55*, 15-40.

Gottfredson, G. D., & Holland, J. L. (1989). *Dictionary of Holland occupational codes* (2nd ed.). Odessa, FL: Psychological Assessment Resources.

Herr, E. L. (1997). Super's life-span, life-space approach and its outlook for refinement. *Career Development Quarterly, 45*, 238-246.

Herr, E. L., & Cramer, S. H. (1996). *Career guidance and counseling through the lifespan: Systematic approaches* (5th ed.). New York: Longman.

Holland, J. L. (1973). *Making vocational choices: A theory of careers*. Englewood Cliffs, NJ: Prentice-Hall.

Holland, J. L. (1982, August). Some *implications of career theory for adult development and aging*. Paper presented at the American Psychological Association, Washington, DC.

Holland, J. L. (1985). *Making vocational choices: A theory of vocational personalities and work environments* (2nd ed.). Englewood Cliffs, NJ: Prentice-Hall.

Holland, J. L. (1992). *Making vocational choices* (2nd ed.). Odessa, FL: Psychological Assessment Resources.

Holland, J. L. (1997). *Making vocational choices* (3rd ed.). Odessa, FL: PsychologicalAssessment Resources.

Holland, J. L., Fritzsche, B. A., & Powell, A. B. (1994). *The Self-Directed Search technical manual.* Odessa, FL: Psychological Assessment Resources.

Holland, J. L., Gottfredson, D. C., & Power, P. G. (1980). Some diagnostic scales and signs for the selection of vocational treatments. *Journal of personality and Social Psychology, 39,*1191-1200.

Holland, J. L., Powell, A. B., & Fritzsche, B. A. (1994). *The Self-Directed Search professional users manual.* Odessa, FL: Psychological Assessment Resources.

Kapes, J. T., & Whitfield, E. A. (Eds.). (2001). *A counselor's guide to career assessment instruments* (4th ed.). Columbus, OH: National Career Development Association.

Lunneborg, P. W., & Westbrook, B. W. (1985). Review of my vocational situation. In J. V. Mitchell, Jr. (Ed.), *9th mental measurements yearbook.* Lincoln, NE: University of Nebraska Press. Retrieved February 20, 2003, from the WEBSPIRS database.

Miller, M. J. (1998). Broadening the use of Holland's hexagon with specific implications for career counselors. *Journal of Employment Counseling, 35,* 2-6.

Niles, S. G., & Harris-Bowlsbey, J. (2002). *Career development interventions in the 21st century.* Upper Saddle River, NJ: Merrill Prentice Hall.

Osipow, S. H., & Fitzgerald, L. F. (1996). *Theories of career development* (4th ed.). Needham Heights, MA: Allyn & Bacon.

Reardon, R. C., & Lenz, J. G. (1999). Holland's theory and career assessment. *Journal of Vocational Behavior, 55,* 102-113.

Sharf, R. S. (2002). *Applying career development theory to counseling* (3rd ed.). Pacific Grove, CA: Brooks/Cole.

Spokane, A. R. (1985). A review of research on person-environment congruence in Holland's theory of careers. *Journal of Vocational Behavior, 28,* 306-343.

U.S. Department of Labor. (n.d.). *Replace with a database O*NET replaces the Dictionary of Occupational Titles.* Retrieved February 21, 2003, from http://www.doleta.gov/programs/onet/onet2txt.asp

Weinrach, S. G., & Srebalus, D. J. (1990). Holland's theory of careers. In D. Brown, L. Brooks, & Associates (Eds.), *Career choice and development* (2nd ed., pp. 37-67). San Francisco: Jossey-Bass.

Yost, E. B., & Corbishley, M. A. (1987). *Career counseling: A psychological approach.* San Francisco: Jossey-Bass.

Zunker, V. G. (2002). *Career counseling: Applied concepts of life planning* (6th ed.). Pacific Grove, CA: Brooks/Cole.

CHAPTER 3

CHAOS OUT OF ORDER

New Perspectives in Career Development in the Information Society

Gary W. Peterson, John D. Krumboltz, and Joseph Garmon

The authors take a unique approach to career theory incorporating chaos theory and applying it to an individual's career development. Case examples are used to illustrate the application of chaos theory to the field of career counseling.

According to many futurists and scholars (Handy, 1994; Rifkin, 1995; Schram & Marshall, 1993; Toffler, 1980; and Toffler & Toffler, 1994), our culture is in a transition from an industrial society to a postindustrial society, or information society. According to Naisbitt (1982), the transformation from an industrial society to an information society is ultimately driven by the dramatic and pervasive forces of technological infusion in all sectors of the labor force, as well as increased global economic development and competition. According to Cascio (1995) and Wegman (1991), the effects of these forces will likely result in (a) changes in the structure of organizations from large, stable, vertically-integrated hierarchies to temporary, interconnected networks of specialized functions, (b)

Issues in Career Development, 53–80

the reengineering of business processes, particularly in the areas of personnel selection, training, rewards, and incentives, (c) a shift from product orientation to customer-service orientation, and (d) a shorter length of job tenure.

Changes in the economy and in business organizations will likely command changes in what, where, and when work will be performed, as well as in career patterns. Standard permanent 40-hour per week jobs with benefits are being replaced by a variety of alternate forms of work. For example, the Bureau of Labor Statistics in 1996 reported that nearly 20% of those employed worked less than 35 hours per week. Part-time workers are used by 72% of organizations (Houseman, 1997). Flextime permits employees to set their own work schedules. Approximately 20% of workers had nonstandard hours in the form of shift work (Hunt, 1994). About 6% of the U.S. labor force engage in moonlighting, for example, holding more than one job at a time (Kimmel, 1995). In 1991, 11 million workers telecommuted at least 1 day per month (Jackson, 1995), and that number is expected to increase to 15 million by the year 2005. (Himmelberg, 1997). According to Polivka (1996), individuals may actually attain a state of being permanently employed as temporary workers. Independent contractors, self-employed workers, free lancers, and consultants are yet other growing alternative forms of employment (Cohany, 1996). Thus, individuals are faced with a variety of choices regarding how they may wish to structure their work lives. Common themes pertaining to changes in careers and career patterns allude to such predictions as job security based on employability rather than on loyalty to an organization, job progression described in terms of career paths rather than career ladders, career choices based on person-environment fit rather than person-job fit, professional credentials functioning more as *hunting licenses* rather than as entitlements or *union cards*, and continuous life-long learning rather than one-time learning and credentialing (Bridges, 1994; Howard, 1995; Shepphard & Carroll, 1980; Wegman, Chapman, & Johnson, 1995). Further, the relationships among work, leisure, interpersonal relationships, community development and spirituality as principal components of life style (Super, 1980) may also undergo dramatic change.

In response to changes in the economy, in work, and in careers, there has been a call for the development of career theory and for redefining the fundamental concepts of job, occupation, career, career development, and career guidance and counseling (Harris-Bowlsbey, 1996; Herr, 1996; Lent, 1996; Watts, 1996). The nature of jobs and careers in an information society may well be described by a different set of concepts, rules, and expectations than the jobs and careers of the industrial society of the last 250 years (Feller, 1991; Samuelson, 1996). In effect, we see a need for a paradigm shift in the way work, jobs, and careers are conceptualized to match the economic revolution taking place in the transformation from the industrial society to the information society (Kuhn, 1978). Ultimately, learning ways to describe, analyze, and understand relationships among work and career phenomena in the information society will enhance adaptability to the new work environment by creating possibilities and opportunities for continuous, productive, satisfying, and meaningful employment.

Therefore, the purpose of this paper is to present elements of a theory of career development by drawing on an emerging theory from mathematics, namely chaos theory, which may help us to understand the complexities of career phenomena in the information society. However, we must emphasize that the objectives of this paper are not to dismiss current theories, to make a case for their irrelevance, or to offer a metatheory that seeks convergence among existing theories (Savickas & Lent, 1994). Instead, we are introducing and applying concepts and metaphors from chaos theory to formulate a new theoretical approach for describing and explaining career behavior in an unpredictable and turbulent work environment of the information society.

A Framework for Theorizing

Theorizing about career development requires a theory about theory. Here, we refer to both the structure and the content of any psychological theory as well as the methods by which one pursues inquiry into a phenomenon (Brown & Brooks, 1996; Slife & Williams, 1997). The specific components of a theory used in this paper are those advanced by Hall and Lindzey (1978) which are (a) assumptions and propositions, (b) concepts and definitions, (c) operations and procedures, and (d) utility and implications for practice and research. These rubrics are herein applied to the development of a theory of career development in an information society. Furthermore, one must be mindful that in this case, we are attempting to understand a phenomenon that is presently unfolding, namely the transition from an industrial society to an information society, a process that began in the 1950s (Toffler, 1980; Toffler & Toffler, 1994). Nevertheless, we believe it is timely to apply the concepts from chaos theory to career development since career counselors are helping individuals to make career decisions and to prepare for and to manage their careers in it. To date, chaos theory has been extended to fields beyond mathematics and natural sciences including psychological systems (Barton, 1994; Masterpasqua, 1997), family systems (Ward, 1995), financial markets (Savit, 1991), teaching (Iannone, 1995; Rockier, 1990–1991), soccer (football) (O'Hare, 1996), sport psychology (Mack, Huddleston, Dutler, & Mintah, 2000), and academic advising (Beck, 1999).

To begin a discussion of a theory of career development several key terms must be defined. *Work* is the exertion of effort toward the attainment of objectives for which there is economic or social worth (see Isaacson & Brown, 1997, pp. 5-10). Four decades ago, Shartle (1959) defined the terms *position*, *job*, and *occupation* that are still appropriate for the information society. A *position* is a circumscribed unit of work tasks performed by an individual in an organization. A *job* is group of similar positions in a single business, whereas an *occupation* is a group of similar jobs across several businesses. An individual engages in a contract with an employer to perform the tasks of a position. In the information society, the performance of tasks comprising a job is often not confined to specific location or regular time frame. Further, at any given time, individuals may engage in contracts with multiple employers to perform the work of several positions in parallel or overlapping time frames. A *career* is the series of paid or unpaid total accumulation of jobs that one performs throughout the life span (Sears, 1982). A *career path* is the linear sequence of jobs mapped out in a time-space continuum, while *career development* is the life-long acquisition of knowledge, interests, cognitive and psychomotor skills, values, beliefs, and talents that under gird the ongoing acquisition and maintenance of productive employment along the career path. Therefore, *a theory of career development* for the information society entails describing a career in terms of a path-dependent phenomenon and then explaining how career paths evolve over time.

The *goal* of a career is to maintain satisfying, productive, and continuous employment within a constantly changing and uncertain work environment. However, career development does not take place in isolation from other facets of life. It entails integrating a career path within the fabric of other concurrent life paths including interpersonal relationships, expression of leisure pursuits, and connectedness and transcendence through community involvement and spiritual dedication. Therefore, the ultimate *aim* or *purpose* of a career is to contribute, as one facet of existence, to a satisfying and meaningful life.

CHAOS THEORY AS A F'OUNDATION FOR UNDERSTANDING CAREER DEVELOPMENT IN THE INFORMATION SOCIETY

Background

As stated above, a theory of career development is needed which possesses descriptive and explanatory power in the work environment of the information society. We propose that concepts and principles of chaos theory (Abraham & Gilgen, 1995; Barton, 1994; Butz, 1997; Cambel, 1993; Gleick, 1988; Robertson & Combs, 1995) provide a useful and comprehensive framework for describing and understanding career path phenomena characterized by nonlinear behavioral patterns across time in a work environment beset by uncertainty and turbulence (Feller & Walz, 1996). The potential usefulness of chaos theory is in its ability to disclose hidden order in nonlinear events that appear random or chaotic on the surface, like eddies in a stream, paths of hurricanes, or even paths of butterflies.

Chaos may be thought of as "a science of patterns, not of predictability" (Chaimberlain, 1995, p. 268), or as "lawless behavior governed by law" (Stewart, 1987, p. 17). At the technical level, chaos theory involves the application of nonlinear dynamic mathematical systems theory and multidimensional fractal geometry to continuous and irregular data sets (e.g., Briggs & Peat, 1989; Devaney, 1987; Glass & Mackey, 1988) and requires advanced vector and differential calculus (Casti, 1985; Mandelbrot, 1977) to develop differential equations to portray inherent patterns in chaotic phenomena. Mathematically, chaotic geometric patterns can be created by taking a single differential equation and using the output as its next input. A nonlinear, nonreoccurring pattern in a two-dimensional space is achieved though adjusting the output at each iteration by a coefficient that never allows the ever continuing plot line to ever repeat exactly the same path (Mandel, 1995). Through such a procedure, while no line in a never-ending path is ever the same, overarching coherent geometric patterns and shapes emerge that might resemble donuts, figure eights, and clovers (Gleick, 1988). A series of differential equations can express chaotic phenomena geometrically in a multidimensional space (Brown, 1995; Lorenz, 1993) as might be called for in mathematically representing collective patterns of work behavior in the present or career-path trajectories over time.

In appropriately applying chaos theory to career phenomena, we believe career paths meet the following necessary characteristics as specified by Heiby (1995): (a) *nonlinearity and irregular periodicity* in which career paths do not conform to linear straight-line trajectories with uniform and timely job transitions along the way; (b) *dynamic in nature* in which internal factors such as learning and maturation interact with external factors such as local and global labor market conditions to determine the next transition along a career path; (c) *bifurcations* in which there are often sudden, unpredictable, and disproportionate changes in the direction and magnitude of job changes along the career path; (d) *sensitivity to initial conditions* (also known as the familiar *butterfly effect*) in which entry into the labor market and transitions from job state to job state along a path are a function of critical early historical antecedents, such as early family experiences or learning in schools; and (e) *self-similarity or magnitude of scale* when career patterns are hierarchically consistent in which both individual and group patterns maintain their same form and structure over time and across scale.

Assumptions

Two fundamental assumptions provide the foundation for the application of chaos theory to individual career-path development.

1. *The future of our culture and the labor market is unpredictable, uncertain, and unknowable*. While futurists may form predictions about the future, we must admit that the future, beyond the immediate time frame, is largely unknowable and conforms to chaotic criteria. We need only to read the *Brave New World* (Huxley, 1932) or *1984*(Orwell, 1949) to realize that forecasts are formed from fantasy, from linear extrapolations of trends formed from an analysis of the past and present, from projections of our dreams or wishes for a better life, and from projections of innate fears of loss of security, status, comforts of the present, or even youth itself (Tierney, 1996).

2. *Careers are path-dependent phenomena*. In the industrial society with a predominance of large hierarchical, monolithic organizations, a typical job progression could be described in terms of a linear *career ladder* in which individuals secured an entry-level job and progressed *upward through the ranks* with each rung promising higher earnings or wages, greater prestige, more perquisites, more job security, and more control over the working environment (Hall & Associates, 1996). However, in an information society, with the continued development of communications technology, organizations will shift toward becoming smaller, flatter, de-centralized, and more temporary entities (Mohrman & Cohen, 1995). In such organizations, job tenure is shortened, and job progression is characterized more by nonlinear *lateral moves* across organizations rather than by *upward* moves within an organization. Therefore, a *career path* is seen as a more appropriate metaphor for describing a progression of jobs throughout the life span in the emerging information age than the *career ladder* of the industrial age. The nature of career paths is that they are unknown until they have been traveled and viewed retrospectively, much like the path of a hurricane. Further, as a chaotic phenomenon, no two individuals ever follow exactly the same path. The starting points, or initial conditions,

are different for each individual as are the steps along the way, since the external environmental conditions and the internal states of individual development at each transition point are also unique.

Concepts and Definitions

The following terms, attractor, work attractor, career path profile, turbulence, bifurcation, and transition are used to describe career-path behavior:

Attractor. A powerful concept borrowed from chaos theory and now applied to career development is that of an *attractor*, which may be considered as a focal point of behavior and energy around which a system gravitates or settles (Briggs & Peat, 1989). There are three kinds of attractors that control and limit an object's range of movement in a system (Thelen, 1989): (1) point attractors, (2) limit-cycle attractors, and (3) strange attractors. A *point attractor* constrains a system around a single gravitational point and attains a steady state or equilibrium. Graphically, it may be portrayed as a donut with lines pivoting circumventing around a single point. A *limit-cycle attractor* constrains a system around predictable repetitive cycles and may be portrayed as a figure eight on its side with lines pivoting around two gravitational points. And finally, a *strange attractor* stretches a system away from convergence around constricting points or cycles and toward divergence around multiple gravitational points. A simple graphical form of a strange attractor with multiple foci may resemble a four-leaf clover with four gravitational points. Strange attractors create unpredictability by drawing a system's vitality into nonprojected patterns of behavior (King, 1991). The three kinds of attractors may be used to describe patterns of work behavior taking place at any point in time along a career path.

Work Attractor. In applying the concept of a chaotic attractor to vocational behavior, we coin the term *work attractor* to connote patterns of work modeled after the properties of chaotic attractors. Patterns of work exemplified by a point attractor may be a standard 40-hour per week job with highly routine and repetitive tasks, as typified by assembly-line work in the industrial age. A pattern of work conforming to a *point attractor* may be viewed as having a single focal point around which work energy and activity gravitates. As a point attractor, a traditional *job* continually draws energy into itself, such that relief from work in days off, holidays, and vacations are joyful, celebrated occasions to restore one's energy and vitality. Retirement with a pension is often viewed as the ultimate relief and end goal of life.

Work patterns modeled after a *limit-cycle attractor* may be characterized by seasonal cycles as experienced by farmers, teachers, and professional athletes. Work tasks vary according to repetitive and predictable cycles in which energy is constrained and regulated according to properties of the cycle. For example, springtime is renewing and energizing for farmers, fall for teachers and winter for professional skiers. The off-season consists of activities associated with preparation and planning for the on-season.

Work patterns conforming to a *strange attractor* involve a constantly changing mix of different kinds of work and work-related activities. The dynamic mix of jobs, managed well, can be constantly energizing and renewing, but if mismanaged, they can be stressful and exhausting. An example of work behavior at the professional level that models a strange attractor may be a counseling psychologist who combines private consultation with individuals under the auspices of a community mental health center for 3 days per week as the primary occupational activity. This commitment is combined with organizational consultation with hospitals and local government agencies, teaching 1 or 2 courses per year as an adjunct faculty member in a local college, and serving as an expert witness in worker disability claims for several law firms. Likewise, an example of a work attractor with the properties of a strange attractor in the skill trades may be an electrician who is employed for an electronic company 30 hours per week, but moonlights on off-hours and off-days, and from time to time, donates service for churches and nonprofit community organizations on a cost-only basis. We believe that work patterns of a growing segment of the labor force in the information society will acquire the complexities of a chaotic strange attractor with multiple gravitational points in varying degrees of flux, which enable the successful adaptation to the ever-shifting demands and opportunities of an information labor market.

Work attractors in the information age not only encompass job-related tasks and duties, but they also include on-going educational and training activities that prepare one for future jobs or for the maintenance of present employment. Furthermore, Tofler and Tofler (1994) and Rifkin (1995) would argue that a work attractor should include both paid and nonpaid work since both supports a life style. Keen (1991) would add that a work attractor should also include work activities that incorporate one's occupation as well as one's vocation. An occupation consists of work activity that one performs to earn a living, whereas a vocation entails work activity, often performed voluntarily without pay that truly enriches and adds meaning to one's life. Thus, the concept of work attractor within the framework of chaos theory encourages individuals to think creatively and holistically about possibilities and opportunities for education and work in terms of an interrelated and coherent array of activities carried out in the pursuit of the realization of one's potential for the good of one's self, significant others, cultural group, and society.

Career path profile. A career path is the dynamic, nonlinear progression through a series of work attractors (rather than *jobs*) across time throughout the life span. A career path, being a path-dependent phenomenon, is characterized by three dimensions, the *time* to progress through a series of work attractors, the *direction* taken at each step, and the *magnitude* of response (Hayes, Blaine, & Meyer, 1995). The magnitude of response, in career terms, alludes to the amount of resources and energy invested in a transition from one work attractor to the next. A simple two-parameter, interest area by time, graph can be used to create a career-path profile in which time is marked along the horizontal axis, and direction, noted in terms of points along Holland's RIASEC typology of interest domains (Holland, 1996), on the vertical axis. Any step along the path (i.e., a work attractor) is determined by its location in time and by the first letter in the Holland Code for the principal job within the attractor. The exact location of a work attractor on the graph can be adjusted upward or downward by the relative importance and influence of secondary sources of employment as perceived holistically by an individual. Through such a graphing procedure individuals may construct their career-path profiles from entry into the labor market until the present. An example of a career-path profile is presented below from a case study (See Figure 3.1).

Transition. The movement from one work attractor to the next is referred to as a *transition* and is brought about by a change in the principal job within the attractor. In terms of chaos theory, the reconstituting of a new attractor from an existing attractor occurs when *turbulence* rises to a critical level causing a *bifurcation* or splitting from the gravitational point(s) of an existing attractor. Bifurcation occurs when the value of a control parameter in a dynamic system exceeds a critical threshold to produce a new chaotic orbit or attractor (Brown, 1995). In career-path development, turbulence, therefore, refers to the destabilization of factors that regulate and control the maintenance of a work attractor at any point in time along a career path. Further, turbulence that threatens to alter the gravitational point of a work attractor may stem from both internal and external sources. Examples of *internal sources* of turbulence include the acquisition of new abilities or capacities, the earning of degrees or certificates, the cultivation of new interests, changes in career or life goals, or the experiencing of discontent or conflict, whereas examples of *external sources* include family changes, spouse transitions, job termination, or the arising of new opportunities in the environment for advancement. Any one or combination of internal or external sources of turbulence could function as control parameters that may stimulate a bifurcation resulting in a transition from an existing work attractor to the formation of a new one.

There are two kinds of transitions resulting from a bifurcation, first order and second order. *First-order* transitions may be thought of as a weakly chaotic consisting of a slow, evolving mix of order and chaos, whereas second order transitions are chaotic, radical, abrupt, and completely unpredictable (Bak & Chen, 1991; Watzlawick, Weakland, & Fish, 1974). First-order transitions in career-path progressions could occur with gradual anticipated changes in internal conditions (normal rate of maturation) or external environmental conditions (family or local economy). An example of a first-order transition would be the completion of a degree program and securing placement in the degree area. *Second-order* catastrophic changes, on the other hand, could result from rapid unexpected internal forces, such as when an individual accidentally incurs a disability, or from external forces such as when an individual suddenly and unpredictably loses the principal job of a work attractor and must replace it with another completely different kind of job to sustain basic needs of life.

Operations and Procedures in Career-Path Development

Turning from concepts and definitions to the operations and dynamics of career path development, the following operations and procedures, consistent with chaos theory, are factors that control and regulate the formation and progression of work attractors throughout the career path. These factors bear on the formation of work attractors as well as the frequency, direction, and magnitude of transitions from one work attractor to the next. Path-regulating mechanisms, work-attractor development, career-path management, and career-path satisfaction form the principal domains of operations and procedures giving coherence and order in career-path development. They are described as follows.

Path-Regulating Mechanisms

Three chaotic principles, initial conditions, self-organizing processes, and connectedness bear on the way career paths are formed and on the way the inevitable transitions are negotiated in maintaining continuous and satisfying employment in an uncertain and unpredictable world of work.

Initial conditions. Known as the familiar *butterfly effect* (Lorenz, 1993) where the flutter of butterfly wings in China could affect the weather in New York, initial conditions refer to the circumstances early in life that dramatically shape the evolution of the career path later in life. Attributes such as the capacity to learn, attitudes toward work, areas of interests and values, resiliency of one's identity, physical strength and endurance, tolerance for risk, family resources, and the extent of one's social network may come to bear in determining the entry point of a career path and in negotiating transitions along the way.

Self-organizing processes. In dynamic systems, the concept of *self-organizing processes* (Waldrop, 1992) alludes to the capacity for actively anticipating environmental change and turning it into an advantage resulting in the ability to recognize and identify career problems, to make choices, and to take action in a planned and timely manner. The acquisition of career problem solving and decision-making skills (Peterson, Sampson, Reardon, & Lenz, 1996, 2002; Reardon, Lenz, Sampson, & Peterson, 2000) and the ability to take advantage of serendipity (Krumboltz, 1998) and happenstance (Mitchell, Levin, & Krumboltz, 1999) are ways to enhance self-organizing processes in dynamic systems. Continuous learning of self-knowledge, world knowledge, as well as cognitive and psychomotor skills enhances one's capability for adaptation to constantly changing market conditions. In addition, the constant development of personality characteristics including interests, values, and self-efficacy are also considered as critical aspects of self-organizing processes.

Connectedness. An important contextual factor exerting an influence on the career-path development is the extent of one's connectedness with significant others, family, ethnic group, professional group, and community. Connectedness alludes to the chaotic principal of *increasing returns* (Robertson & Combs, 1995), which refers to the exponential relationship between the number of linkages in one's communication network and returns in the form of information, in this case knowledge about occupations and job prospects. We would also add that connectedness entails social support and encouragement as well as countervailing forces of resistance and discouragement (Lent, Brown, & Hackett, 2000). Thus, opportunities for the development of work attractors as well as the opportunities to embark on growth transitions are directly influenced according to the extent and quality of one's social network.

Steering currents. These are emergent themes, derived from an analysis of initial conditions and transitions, which provide coherence and order to a career path. Interests, abilities, values, and opportunities as initial conditions set the path in motion in the early stages of career path development. Then, as time progresses, a higher-order, perhaps spiritual, purpose emerges that focuses the career path. Some would view this process as responding to one's calling (Huntley, 1997; Keen, 1991; Rayburn, 1997). Examples of emergent themes allude to the pursuit of congruence between one's dominant interest and the type of environment of the principal job within an attractor, the importance of continued support and encouragement by a significant other, or the extent of fulfillment in an ultimate purpose or meaning in work.

Work-Attractor Development

As stated above, a work attractor serves as a dynamic gravitational point of life energy and activity. Modeled after the properties of a chaotic attractor, a work attractor may vary in complexity from a simple point-attractor with a single gravitational point (e.g., a single 40-hour per week job) to a limit-cycle attractor with polar opposite gravitational points (e.g., on- off-seasonal work), to a complex strange attractor with multiple subgravitational points (e.g., several part-time jobs, education, volunteer work). We like to think of the process of creating work attractors as analogous to a traditional family farmer deciding which combination of crops and livestock will produce the highest sustainable yield given the quality and amount of land at hand given local and global commodities market conditions. Likewise, in creating a work attractor, the commodities are one's marketable skills and knowledge to be actualized through a job or a mix of jobs in a local labor market. The aggregate of jobs and education comprising the work attractor should optimize the use of one's abilities and talents to form the most satisfying and sustainable level of productivity.

Career-Path Management

In order to manage a career path (i.e., progression of work attractors across a time span), individuals must acquire a set of skills, knowledge, and attitudes beyond those required to make appropriate job choices at any point along a career path. Career-path management demands a capacity for self-organizing criticality (Waldrop, 1992), the ability to maintain a strong sense of personal identity, purpose, and direction in the midst of a near-chaotic environment (Bak & Chen, 1991). It also requires a constant vigilance of changing economic patterns in the local and global markets in one's career field, the ever-present weighing of possibilities and opportunities to alter the composition of one's work attractor, and the capacity to make judgments pertaining to when or when not to modify the job mix within a work attractor (Janis & Mann, 1977). Effective career-path management requires the fortitude to resist the seductive temptation of striving to create and maintain low-risk comfort zones of security and predictability (Marion, 1994).

In some respects, career-path management requires the thought processes and skills possessed by expert pool or chess players. Take for example pool players. Novice pool players focus exclusively on hitting the target ball with the cue ball in such a way as to enable the target ball to hit a designated pocket. After contact, should the target ball hit a pocket, they then prepare for the next shot from where ever the cue ball happens to finish. Experts, on the other hand, focus not only on the cue ball and the target ball, but also contemplate the speed and the spin the cue ball must attain so that it not only hits the target ball into the intended pocket, but that it also comes to a stop on the table so as to be situated in an ideal position for the next shot. In the same manner, skillful career-path management requires not only planning and preparing for the immediate next job, but also how that job could position one's self for the next move along the path. Such skills enable individuals to anticipate and prepare for changes in the environment as well as to be sensitive and open to new opportunities when they arise (Krumboltz, 1998; Mitchel, Levin, & Krumboltz, 1999).

Finally, career path management also necessitates, for those in committed relationships, the ability to coordinate one's own career path with the path of a partner to form joint attractors that may acquire the properties of limit-cycle or strange attractors. In managing dual paths, there may be times when both are fully employed, other times when one is fully employed and the other partially or not employed, and yet other times when both are not fully employed. Thus, an important aspect of career-path management in committed relationships entails orchestrating two paths as complementary components of a single work attractor while looking to one another for emotional support and opportunities for learning.

Career-Path Satisfaction

The outcome of effective work attractor development and career path management is a satisfying and productive career. While there has been research concerning job satisfaction and the relationship between satisfaction and job performance at any point in time (Iaffaldino & Muchinsky, 1985; Katzell, 1980; Petty, McGee, & Cavender, 1984), there has been little if any research concerning career-path satisfaction or its relationship to productivity or associated variables such as self-esteem or general life adjustment. Further, job satisfaction has typically been measured in terms of instruments such as the *Minnesota Satisfaction Questionnaire* (Weiss, Dawis, England, & Lofquist, 1967), which assess overall satisfaction along with levels of satisfaction with aspects of a given job. The assessment of career-path satisfaction, however, entails unique challenges since a work attractor at any point in time may involve multiple jobs and a career path is comprised of an evolving series of work attractors over an extended period of time.

For this paper, career-path satisfaction is defined in terms of the recollection of one's state of happiness (Csikszentmihalyi, 1999; Fordyce, 1988) with a work attractor at any point along a career path. Career-path satisfaction at any time is represented by point on a continuous trace line extended over time that varies on a 5-point continuum, where +2 = highly satisfied, +1 = moderately satisfied, 0 = neutral, –1 = moderately dissatisfied and –2 = highly dissatisfied (See Figure 2). The identification of path themes and steering currents governing one's career-path satisfaction emerge by first conducting an analysis of factors associated with initial conditions along with each transition in a career path. Then a continuous trace line is constructed which expresses the level of satisfaction with one's career path from entry to the present. Logical associations are then made between path-regulating mechanisms involved in transitions (i.e., initial conditions, turbulence, bifurcation, connectedness) and satisfaction along the path.

Application and Utility

To illustrate how chaos theory can be applied to describing and understanding career-path phenomena, the case of Marlene (pseudonym) is presented whose career path illuminates many of the above terms and concepts. In conducting the study, qualitative research methods (Maxwell, 1996) were used for exploring phenomena that are not clearly defined or when an area of inquiry is in its incipient stages of development. The approach was similar to the phenomenological inquiry employed by Brooks and Daniluk (1998) in observing the career paths of women artists. The third author conducted both an initial structured interview and a follow-up interview with Marlene.

THE CASE OF MARLENE

Marlene is a 42-year-old divorced African American woman who is employed as a private-practice psychiatrist in a medium-sized town in the southeast. She has one 6-year-old son.

Initial conditions. Initial conditions prior to embarking on her career path were assessed in terms of (a) *opportunity*, the resources provided by her family, (b) *abilities*, academic skills and capacity to learn, (c) *interests*, dominant interest areas as reflected by her recollection of career aspirations, and (d) *connectedness*, communication linkages beyond the home that provide occupational information, guidance, encouragement, and knowledge of job prospects.

Opportunity. Marlene's father possessed a doctor of divinity degree and served as a pastor of a church at the time she left high school. Her mother was a high school graduate and worked full time as a cosmetologist. Marlene described her family as middle class. While, both of Marlene's parents wanted her to attend college, they had no specific expectations regarding a career choice.

Abilities. Marlene recalled that her high school GPA was about 3.5 on a 4.0 scale and that her class rank was in the upper half. Marlene said she knew she had the ability to be successful in college.

Interests. At the time of high school graduation, Marlene's aspirations included a dietitian (Holland Code SIE) and an owner of a nursing home (Holland Code SER). At the time of the initial interview in the present, Marlene's measured Holland Code employing The Self-Directed Search (Holland, 1994) was SEA. At the time she left high school, Marlene did not recall having any specific hobbies and that most of her leisure time was devoted to involvement with the church.

Connectedness. Marlene's maternal aunt was a dietitian who was well respected by the family. An important influence in Marlene's life was "a white woman who was like a Godmother to me" and encouraged her to become a doctor. This woman was a member of the country club where Marlene worked as a part-time cook after school. At this time, Marlene was experiencing "terrible times" at home because of conflicts with her family over leaving the denomination in which her father pastured. She said she placed much emphasis on the influence of this particular woman because of the alienation she felt with her family.

Marlene's career path. Marlene's career path profile is presented in Figure 1 in which time is marked along the horizontal axis and points of the Holland Hexagon on the vertical axis. The placement of any work attractor on the graph is located according to the principal job of a work attractor along with the relative influence of other paid and nonpaid work comprising the attractor. Marlene along with the interviewer located each attractor on Figure 1.

Work attractor #1 (WA1). The principal job of WA1 consisted of a short-order cook at a country club (RSE). She obtained this job in her senior year in high school and held the position for 2 years. After graduation from high school, WA1 possessed the characteristics of a point attractor with work activities gravitating around a single point.

Transition from Work Attractor # 1 (WA1) to Work Attractor #2 (WA2). The turbulence driving the change from WA1 to WA2 stemmed from both internal and external sources. Internally, Marlene knew that working as a cook was not a job on which to build a career, but she did not have a clear career goal in mind. Externally, she experienced conflict with her family over her church membership and the relationship with her boyfriend had become abusive. At the same time, she was encouraged by her "Godmother" to attend college and to pursue becoming a medical doctor. Marlene decided to relocate to another state to escape conflicts in her life as well as to pursue a college degree. Her career aspiration at the time was to become a high school science teacher although she held on to the possibility of pursuing medicine. Thus, this transition was propelled by both internal and external turbulence and she possessed control over the change. However, because of the dramatic and sudden departure from an existing attractor to a completely different attractor, the bifurcation was considered a second-order change. Ironically, Marlene viewed the transition as a negative event in her life because of the degree of emotional turmoil surrounding the change.

Work attractor #2 (WA2). The principal job that formed WA2 was performing as a student majoring in science education (SAE). To support herself financially, she secured secondary employment as a part-time librarian assistant (CSE) and held this job as a work-study student. During this time, Marlene became involved in campus ministry and performed leadership roles. She also became involved in campus social action groups and developed a keen interest in the needs of minorities and underprivileged. She said she began developing a black consciousness. Thus WA2 conformed to the properties of a strange attractor with multiple gravitational points, for example, science education major, library assistant, campus ministry leader, social activist, and advocate for African Americans. Marlene attended undergraduate school for 4 years.

Transition: WA2 to WA3. The turbulence that precipitated the transition from WA2 to WA3 was graduation from college resulting in the termination of employment as a librarian assistant. To support herself financially while seeking employment as a teacher, Marlene took a job as short-order cook in a local restaurant (RSE) on finding the job through a local newspaper. Thus, external forces drove the transition from WA2 to WA3. Because she anticipated job termination well in advance, and she formed a new attractor with a principal job with which she was familiar, the bifurcation is viewed as a first-order change. Since she did not like the work of a short-order cook, Marlene viewed the transition as negative. Finally, in terms of connectedness, she was unsure of whether to pursue a teaching job or apply for medical school, and did not feel there was anyone to guide her.

Work attractor #3 (WA3). The principal job of WA3 was again a short-order cook (RSE). Marlene held this job for 3 months. During this time she continued to be actively involved in the campus ministry. The temporary, singular work of WA3 made it a point attractor.

Transition: WA3 to WA4. The turbulence promoting the change from WA3 to WA4 was a combination of dissatisfaction with the job of short-order cook and the opportunity of being offered a job as a full-time substitute science teacher (SAE) in a local high school. This change is viewed as a first-order change since Marlene was well prepared for the shift, viewed the job as a short-order cook in WA3 as temporary employment and was anticipating a transition to form a new attractor as soon as possible. She also received approval from her parents and her college professors.

Work attractor #4 (WA4). Serving as a high school science teacher formed the principal job of WA4. Marlene remained in this job for 3 years. During this time, she became involved with young professionals and older graduate students in her church. In terms of connectedness, she began teaching a high school class at church and became involved with other African American professionals in informal social activist groups. Marlene also worked as a campaign volunteer for an African American who was running for city council. Thus, serving as a teacher with on-season, off-season work could have resulted in the development of a limit-cycle attractor. However, because of Marlene's involvement in multiple paid and unpaid work activities, WA4 acquired the properties of a strange attractor.

Transition: WA4 to WA5. After an initial liking of her job as a high school science teacher, Marlene grew to dislike it. She felt disrespected by her principal, and that the occupation of high school teacher failed to provide a sense of worth and esteem she desired. During this time, she again began to entertain the idea of becoming a doctor (IRS) although she had not formulated a specialization. In terms of connectedness, her peers at both her church and in her political activist activities provided encouragement and support to pursue a career in medicine. During the third year of teaching she applied to medical school and was accepted with a fellowship. Thus, the turbulence was in the form of both a push (she disliked her work) and a pull (she perceived opportunity for fulfillment in the medical field). She viewed the transition positively. Since the change was gradual and planned, the bifurcation was a first order change. She was investing her social and investigative interests and abilities in a new direction along her career path.

Work attractor #5 (WA5). While in medical school, she pursued becoming a general practitioner. Even though there were considerable demands placed on her in medical school, she still found time for involvement in a social political group, International Physicians for Prevention of Nuclear War. Thus, work activities of WA5 pivoted around two distinct polar gravitational points making it a limit cycle attractor. Marlene attended medical school for 4 years.

Transition: WA5 to WA6. Graduation from medical school served as the source of turbulence that moved her on to form WA6, which included serving as a Nobel Emissary for International Physicians for Prevention of Nuclear War (SEA). Marlene saw this position as one in which she could "do something to make the world a safer place and by reducing poverty and suffering." This transition was again both a push (graduation) and a pull (the desire to exercise her social interest). She viewed the transition positively. This was a first-order change because it was anticipated and occurred over a span of time.

Work attractor #6 (WA6). The primary job of WA6 was a Nobel Emissary (SEA), which entailed visiting Third World nations to help them draft foreign policy. She also interacted with medical personnel in these countries and interacted with agencies that provided support to the poor. During her work as an emissary, she served as a medical missionary for various church groups, often providing her own financial support. In addition, she formed her own nonprofit organization, Pyramids of Hope, to "make a difference in lives of poor people." Marlene held the position emissary for 4 years. Again, Marlene created a work attractor with the attributes of a strange attractor with multiple gravitational points, emissary, medical missionary, and corporate leader of a nonprofit organization.

Transition: WA6 to WA7. While serving as an emissary, Marlene grew to wanting to practice medicine as a psychiatrist in order to "help people who are hurting." In addition, the funds to support her work as an emissary expired. She secured a residency program to provide the necessary training in psychiatry (ISA). Regarding connectedness, the city in which she was to become a resident was also the same city in which a new boyfriend was moving. Thus, the turbulence promoting the change was both internal, stemming from a desire to pursue meaningful work and relationship opportunities, as well as external, termination of funds to support the primary job of WA6. Because this change evolved over the span of a year and was viewed as finding a new outlet for her social and investigative interests, the bifurcation entailed a first-order change. She viewed the transition in a positive light.

Work attractor #7 (WA7). Marlene's tenure as a psychiatric resident (WA7) lasted for 1 year. Since this was her single and only work activity, WA7 was a point attractor.

Transition: WA7 to WA8. On completion of the residency, Marlene found a position as a psychiatrist (ISA) in a hospital in another community. The turbulence fostering this change was both external with the termination of the residency and internal in that she sought new opportunity to practice medicine. At the same time the relationship with her boyfriend soured. Again the transition was anticipated and planned. Thus, the bifurcation resulted in a first-order change.

Work attractor #8 (WA8). Marlene served as psychiatrist (ISA) in the hospital for 3 years (WA8). She also married during this time, had a child, and was divorced. While Marlene lived with her husband, they shared a joint limit-cycle attractor in which she was providing financial support for him to attend school. She found this joint limit-cycle attractor unsatisfactory.

Transition: WA8 to WA9. Marlene grew to dislike her job as a psychiatrist because of broken promises, being assigned undesirable tasks in the hospital, as well as experiencing racial and gender discrimination. She decided to pursue independent practice as a psychiatrist (ISA). Turbulence under girding the transition was created through an untenable job situation as well as relationship difficulties. Because of the unpleasantness of the circumstances, she viewed the transition as negative. This was a first-order transition.

Work attractor #9 (WA9). Marlene has maintained a private practice as a psychiatrist for 5 years (WA9). A contract with the Department of Juvenile Justice forms a core component for her practice. Her practice also includes individual walk-in clients from the community, and consultation with schools regarding children and youth with learning disabilities. Much of her consultation with schools is on a *pro bono* basis. Thus, she has created a strange work attractor with multiple gravitational points. She is an active member of a local church in which she serves as an elder. In addition, she has formed a new significant relationship, but he is contemplating job offers out-of-state. Marlene is unsure of whether she will move with him or remain in her present circumstance.

Career Path Satisfaction

Marlene's recollection of career path satisfaction (Figure 3.2) reveals that she was largely dissatisfied with her work in attractors 1 through 4 in which she held primary jobs within the respective work attractors of short order cook (RSE), science education major (ISA), short order cook (RSE), and high school science teacher (SEA). Work satisfaction did not cross the neutral line and into the positive area until attractor 5 when she attended medical school (IRS). Work attractor 6, whose primary job was Nobel Emissary (SEA), was viewed as a positive experience along with attractor 7 when she returned to school as psychiatric resident (ISA). The 1-year attractor 8 as a psychiatrist (ISA) in a hospital was viewed negatively. The present work attractor 9 as a private practice psychiatrist (ISA) over the past 5 years is viewed as increasingly positive.

Themes and Steering Currents Governing Marlene's Career Path

Several themes emerge that appear to provide coherence and order in Marlene's path:

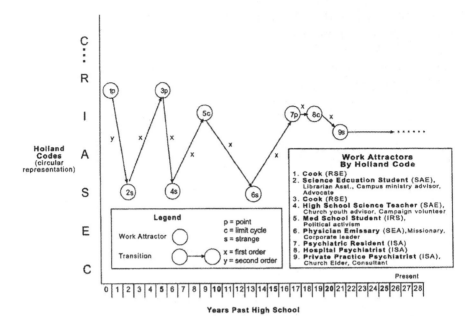

Figure 3.1.   Career-path profile of Marlene.

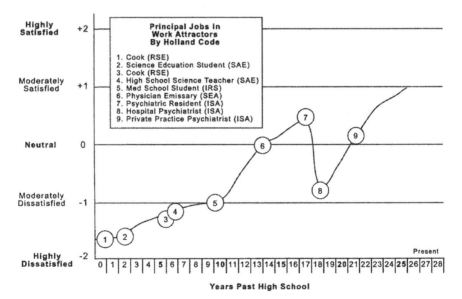

Figure 3.2.   Trace line of work satisfaction by Marlene.

- The striving to enhance her feeling of self-worth through educational and occupational advancement;
- The need to overcome social and institutional discrimination, prejudice, and injustice;
- The strong need for autonomy and independence;
- The need to fulfill a spiritual calling of making a positive difference in the world through her compassion for the underprivileged;
- The desire to share her career path with a partner one; and
- A work attractor with multiple gravitational points (strange attractor) along with active participation in church and a committed relationship appear to provide the optimal conditions for work satisfaction.

Thus, the case of Marlene demonstrates how chaos theory illuminates certain aspects of her career behavior in which career development is expressed in terms of a path-dependent phenomenon. Concepts such as initial conditions, turbulence, transitions, attractor, connectedness, and first and second-order change are used to describe the forces that influence the impetus, direction, and magnitude of change along her path. Finally, steering currents (emergent themes) provide coherence and order in seemingly random behavior as well as conditions that foster satisfaction in her work.

A Chaotic Research Agenda

With such fundamental changes in the nature of work and career development processes in the information society, the important theoretical question arises, what are the implications for research in career development? We have found that chaos theory easily stimulates a plethora of questions and possibilities for inquiry that could push the frontiers of knowledge in understanding career-path behavior. Three domains of research are proposed to frame the agenda: normative studies, work attractor studies, and career path studies.

Normative studies. These studies pursue the possibility that there are certain career path norms or types that emerge given certain initial parameters (x, y, z) and modified by phase-space parameters (s, r, b) using a series of differential equations. Normative patterns of career paths can be used as possible predictors of career path development given certain parameters of initial and phase space conditions. Initial parameters might include interests, abilities, educational attainments, and early family characteristics or circumstances while phase space parameters along a time continuum might include educational attainment, changes in relationship or family status, and economic status (e.g., average job tenure). With a sufficiently large database such as census data available at the national or state levels, differential equations can be derived to map various time series trajectories as the respective variables are systematically manipulated (Brown, 1995).

Given the chaos principle of *self-similarity* in which parts of a system maintain the same structure as wholes, studies of lesser scale, but yet structurally consistent with large-scale studies, might include the career-path trajectories of members of well-defined cohort groups. For example, we have much to learn from observing career trajectories of valedictorians (Arnold, 1995), or observing subsets of a high school graduating cohort whose dominant interests were in a specific interest domain (e.g., Realistic in the Holland scheme), or comparing initial interests and career trajectories of identical and fraternal twins and siblings of intact families.

Work Attractor Studies. These studies concern factors that influence the composition and productivity of work attractors as they ultimately relate to work satisfaction and the quality of life. Here, the focus is on the phase state of an attractor at a given point along a career path. Inquiry questions that come immediately to mind include: If the mix of jobs comprising a work attractor can be thought of as analogous to the mix of livestock and crops of a traditional family farm, what are the mixes of paid and unpaid, part time or full time, or standard or alternative employment that maximizes productivity and satisfaction? Are dominant interests necessarily coupled with the primary employment of an attractor to render high degrees of satisfaction, or can dominant interests be relegated to secondary employment without loss of satisfaction in the work attractor as a holistic entity? In committed relationships with a joint work attractor, what mixes of standard and alternative employment optimize productivity, work satisfaction and relationship harmony?

Career Path Studies. Studies in this area concern the investigation of factors that influence the rate, direction, and magnitude of changes in work attractors along a career path. Examples of questions stimulated by the application of chaos theory to career development include: What sudden and catastrophic changes in internal and external states precipitate a sudden bifurcation as opposed to gradual evolutionary shifts? What are the relationships among selected personality variables such as self-efficacy, interest structure, human abilities, or personality structure and the rate, direction, and magnitude of career change along a career path? To what extent does the holding of standard employment function as a suppresser variable in the creation of work attractor job diversity or the rate, direction, and magnitude of change along a career path?

SUMMARY AND CONCLUSION

As we move inexorably closer toward the realization of the information society of the twenty-first century, the nature of the economy, the labor force, organizations, careers, jobs and workplace will continue to evolve. According to forecasts (Cohany, 1996; Polivka, 1996), there will be an appreciable increase in alternative forms of employment with respect to the standard 40-hour per week job. Individual survival may be contingent on one's capability to creatively combine several jobs simultaneously along with elements of paid and nonpaid work to form work attractors that sustain a productive and satisfying life style. In the emerging work environment, the metaphor of career path may be a more appropriate representation of the career development process than the metaphor of career ladder. A theory of career development was introduced employing chaos theory as a conceptual framework for describing career-path phenomena using such terms as attractor, sensitivity to initial conditions, turbulence, bifurcation, transition, connectedness, and self-organizing processes.

The use of graphs and figures were introduced as important mechanisms to portray chaotic career phenomena. A two-parameter graphing technique was introduced for mapping an individual career path using the Holland model and was demonstrated through a case study. The use of a trace line to portray work satisfaction over time was used to derive themes and steering currents that ostensibly under gird career path development and ultimately work satisfaction in the case of Marlene. Both of these techniques have potential utility for career counseling and career assessment. Further, chaotic concepts and assessment techniques could serve as the foundation for the development of a theory of career counseling whose ultimate goal would be the attainment of productive work attractors and satisfying career paths.

Areas of research that could be explored to understand career-path phenomena may focus on the development of quantitative and qualitative research methods (Brown, 1995; Hayes, Blame, & Meyer, 1995; Mandel, 1995) to investigate factors that influence career path behavior. A research agenda stimulated by application of chaos theory to career development included normative studies to investigate overarching societal patterns or types of career paths given certain initial conditions and control parameters; work attractor studies to examine factors that govern the formation, continuation, and demise of work attractors; and career path studies that investigate factors that influence the development of individual career paths. Such information may be useful in helping individuals to successfully manage their career paths.

In conclusion, we believe the concepts and principles taken from chaos theory can advance the understanding of the complexities of career development in the new work environment along with awareness of the opportunities the new work environment holds for the creation of a productive and satisfying work life.

REFERENCES

Abraham, F. D., & Gilgen, A. R. (Eds.). (1995). *Chaos theory in psychology.* Westport, CT: Greenwood Press.

Arnold, K. D. (1995). *Lives of promise.* San Francisco: Jossey-Bass.

Bak, P., & Chen, K. (1991, January). Self-organized criticality. *Scientific American,* pp. 46-53.

Barton, S. (1994). Chaos, self-organization, and psychology. *American Psychologist, 49,* 747-755.

Beck, A. (1999, Spring). Advising undecided students: Lessons from chaos theory. *NACADA Journal, 19,* 45-49.

Bridges, W. (1994). *Job shift: How to prosper in a workplace without jobs.* Reading, MA: Addison-Wesley.

Briggs, J., & Peat, F. D. (1989). *Turbulent mirror: An illustrated guide to chaos theory and the science of wholeness.* New York: Harper & Row.

Brooks, G. S., & Daniluk, J. C. (1998). Creative labor: The lives and careers of women artists. *Career Development Quarterly, 47,* 103-118.

Brown, C. (1995). *Chaos and catastrophe theories.* Thousand Oaks, CA: Sage.

Brown, D., & Brooks, L. (1996). Introduction to theories of career development and choice: Origins, evolution, and current efforts. In D. Brown, L. Brooks, & Associates (Eds.), *Career choice and development* (4th ed., pp. 1-30). San Francisco: Jossey-Bass.

Butz, M. R. (1997). *Chaos and complexity theory: Implications for psychological theory and practice.* Washington, DC: Taylor & Francis.

Cambel, A. B. (1993). *Applied chaos theory: A paradigm for complexity.* Boston: Academic Press.

Cascio, W. F. (1995). Whither industrial and organizational psychology in a changing world of work. *American Psycholgist, 50,* 928-939.

Casti, J. L. (1985). *Non linear systems theory.* New York: Academic Press.

Chaimberlain, L. (1995). Strange attractors-patterns in family interaction. In R. Robertson & A. Combs (Eds.), *Chaos theory in psychology and the life sciences.* Mahwah, NJ: Erlbaum.

Csikszentmihalyi, M. (1999). If we are so rich, why aren't we happy? *American Psychologist, 54,* 82, 1-827.

Cohany, S. R. (1996, October). Workers in alternative employment arrangements. *Monthly Labor Review,* pp. 31-45.

Devaney, R. L. (1987). *An introduction to chaotic dynamical systems.* New York: Harper & Row.

Feller, R. (1991). Employment and career development in a world of change: What is ahead for the next twenty-five years? *Journal of Employment Counseling, 25,* 13-20.

Feller, R., & Walz, G. (Eds). (1996). *Career transitions in turbulent times: Exploring work, learning and careers.* Greensboro, NC: ERIC/CASS.

Fordyce, M. W. (1988). A review of research on the happiness measures: A sixty-second index of happiness and mental health. *Social Indicators Research, 20,* 355-381.

Glass, L., & Mackey, M. C. (1988). *From clocks to chaos.* Princeton, NJ: Princeton University Press.

Gleick, J. (1988). *Chaos: Making of a new science.* New York: Penguin Books.

Hall, C. S., & Lindzey, G. (1978). *Theories of personality* (3rd ed.). New York: John Wiley.

Hall, D. C., & Associates (1996). *The career is dead ... long live the career.* San Francisco: Jossey-Bass.

Handy, C. (1994). *The empty raincoat: Making sense of the future.* London: Hutchenson.

Harris-Bowlsbey, J. (1996). Synthesis and antithesis: Perspectives from Herr, Block, and Watts. *Career Development Quarterly, 45,* 54-57.

Hayes, S. N., Blame, D., & Meyer, K. (1995). Dynamic models for psychological assessment: Phase-space functions. *Psychological Assessment, 7,* 17-24.

Heiby, E. M. (1995). Assessment of behavioral chaos with a focus on transitions in depression. *Psychological Assessment, 7,* 10-16.

Herr, E. L. (1996). Perspectives on ecological context, social policy, and career guridance. *Career Development Quarterly, 45,* 5-19.

Himmelberg, M. (1997, March 30). Telecommuting carves out a niche. *Tallahassee Democrat,* p. 1C.

Holland, J. L. (1994). *Self-Directed Search form R* (4th ed.). Odessa, FL: Psychological Assessment Resources.

Holland, J. I.. (1996). Exploring careers with a typology. *American Psychologist, 51,* 397-406.

Houseman, S. M. (1997, Spring). New institute survey on flexible staffing arrangements. *Employment Research, 4*(1), 1, 3-4

Howard, A. (Ed.). (1995). *The changing nature of work.* San Francisco: Jossey-Bass.

Hunt, K. (1994, May 10). Good luck finding after-hours day care. *Tallahassee Democrat,* p. 9D.

Huntley, H. L. (1997). How does "God talk" speak in the workplace?: An essay on the theology of work. In D. P. Bloch & L. J. Richmond (Eds.), *Connections between spirit and work in career development* (pp. 115-136). Palo Alto, CA: Davies-Black.

Huxley, A. (1932). *Brave new world.* New York: Harper & Row.

Iaffaldino, M. T., & Muchinsky, P. M. (1995). Job satisfaction and performance: A metaanalysis. *Psychological Bulletin, 97*(25), 1-273.

Iannone, R. (1995). Chaos theory and its implications for curriculum and teaching. *Education, 115,* 541-547.

Isaacson, L. E., & Brown, D. (1997). *Career information, career counseling and career development* (6th ed.). Needham Heights, MA: Allyn & Bacon.

Jackson, M. (1995, July 3). Despite some manager resistance, telecommuting starts to take hold. *Tallahassee Democrat*, p. 6B.

Janis, I. J., & Mann, L. (1977). *Decision making: A psychological analysis of conflict, choice, and commitment*. New York: Free Press.

Katzell, R. A. (1980). Work attitudes, motivators, and performance. *Professional Psychology, 11*, 409-420.

Keen, S. (1991). *Fire in the belly: On being a man*. New York: Bantam Books.

Kimmel, J. (1995, Spring). Moonlighting in the United States. *Employment Research, 2*(1), 4-6.

King, J. W. (1991, April). Chaos, communication, and educational technology. Paper presented at the annual meeting of the Association for Educational Communications and Technology, Orlando, Fl.

Krumboltz, J. D. (1998). Serendipity is not serendipitous. *Journal of Counseling Psychology, 45*, 390-392.

Kuhn, T. S. (1978). *The structure of scientific revolutions* (2nd ed.). Chicago: University of Chicago Press.

Lent, R. W. (1996). Career counseling, service, and policy: Revitalizing our paradigms and roles. *Career Development Quarterly, 45*, 58-64.

Lent, R. W., Brown, S. D., & Hackett, G. (2000). Contextual supports and barriers to career choice: A social cognitive analysis. *Journal of Counseling Psychology, 47*, 36-49.

Lorenz, E. N. (1993). Deterministic non-periodic flow. *Journal of Atmospheric Science, 20*, 130-141.

Mack, M. G., Huddleston, S., Dutler, K. S., & Mintah, J. K. (2000). Chaos theory: A new science for sport behavior? *Athletic Insight: The Online Journal Of Sport Psychology*. http://www.athleticInsight.com/chaosTheoryFrame1source1.html

Mandel, D. R. (1995). Chaos theory, sensitive dependence and the logistic equation. *American Psychologist, 50*, 106-107.

Mandelbrot, B. B. (1977). *The fractal geometry of nature*. New York: Freeman.

Marion, P. (1994). *Crisis-proof your career*. New York: Berkely.

Masterpasqua, F. (1997). Toward a dynamical development of understanding of disorder. In F. Masterpasqua & P. A. Perna (Eds.), *The psychological meaning of chaos* (pp. 23-40). Washington DC: American Psychological Association.

Maxwell, J. A. (1996). *Qualitative research design: An interactive approach*. Newbury Park, CA: Sage.

Mitchell, K. E., Levin, A. S., & Krumboltz, J. D. (1999). Planned happenstance: Constructing unexpected career opportunities. *Journal of Counseling and Development, 77*, 115-124.

Mohrman, S. A., & Cohen, S. G. (1995). When people get out of the box: New relationships, new systems. In A. Howard (Ed.), *The changing nature of work* (pp. 365-410). San Francisco: Jossey-Bass.

Naisbitt, S. (1982). *Megatrends: Ten new directions in transforming our lives*. New York: Warner Books.

O'Hare, M. (1996). Chaos pitch: Applications of chaos theory to football matches. *New Scientist, 150*(2033), 24-28.

Orwell, G. (1949). *1984*. New York: Harcourt, Brace & Company.

Peterson, G. W., Sampson, J. P. Jr., Reardon, R. C., & Lenz, J. G. (1996). A cognitive information processing approach to career problem solving and decision making. In D. Brown & L. Brooks (Eds.), *Career choice and development* (3rd ed., pp. 423-475*)*. San Francisco: Jossey-Bass.

Peterson, G. W., Sampson, J. P. Jr., Reardon, R. C., & Lenz, J. G. (2002). A cognitive information processing approach to career problem solving and decision making. In D. Brown (Ed.), *Career choice and development* (4th ed.) San Francisco: Jossey-Bass.

Petty, M. M., McGee, G. W., & Cavender, J. W. (1984). A meta-analysis of the relationships between individual job satisfaction and individual performance. *Academy of Management Review, 9,* 712-721.

Polivka, A. E. (1996, October). Contingent and alternative work arrangements defined. *Monthly Labor Review,* pp. 3-9.

Rayburn, C. A. (1997). Vocation as calling: Affirmative response or "wrong number?" In D. P. Bloch & L. J. Richmond (Eds.), *Connections between spirit and work in career development* (pp. 163-184). Palo Alto, CA: Davies-Black.

Reardon, R. C., Lenz, J. G., Sampson, J. P. Jr., & Peterson, G. W. (2000). *Career planning and development: A comprehensive approach.* Belmont, CA: Brooks/Cole.

Rifkin, J. (1995). *Decline of the global labor force and the dawn of the post-market era.* New York: Tardier/Putnam.

Robertson, R., & Combs, A. (Eds.). (1995). *Chaos theory in psychology and the life sciences.* Mahwah, NJ: Erlbaum.

Rockier, M. J. (1990-1991). Thinking about chaos: Non-quantitative approaches to teacher education. *Theory and Practice, 12*(4), 56-62.

Samuelson, R. J. (1996, January 8). Great expectations: The post-war paradox. *Newsweek, 127*(2), 24-34.

Savickas, M. S., & Lent, R. W. (1994). *Convergence in career development theory: Implications for science and practice.* Palo Alto, CA: Davies-Black.

Savit, R. E. (1991). Chaos on the trading floor. In N. Hall (Ed.), *Exploring chaos: A guide to the new science of disorder* (pp. 174-183). New York: W. W. Norton.

Schram, M., & Marshall, W. (1993). *Mandate for change.* New York: Berkely Books.

Sears, S. (1982). A definition of career guidance terms. A National Vocational Guidance Association perspective. *The Vocational Guidance Quarterly, 13,* 137-143.

Shartle, C. L. (1959). *Occupational information—Its development and application* (3rd ed.). Englewood Cliffs, NJ: Prentice-Hall.

Shepphard, C. S., & Carroll, D. C. (1980). *Working in the twenty-first century.* New York: John Wiley.

Slife, B. D., & Williams, R. N. (1997). Toward a theoretical psychology. *American Psychologist, 52,* 117-129.

Stewart, I. (1987). *Does God play dice? The mathematics of chaos.* New York: Basil Blackwell.

Super, D. E. (1980). A life-span, life space approach to career development. *Journal of Vocational Development, 27,* 282-298.

Thelen, E. (1989). Self-organization in developmental processes: Can systems approaches work? In M. R. Gunnar & E. Thelen (Eds.), *Systems and develop-*

ment (pp. 77-115). The Minnesota Symposium on Child Psychology. Hillsdale, NJ: Erlbaum.

Tierney, J. (1996). Future phobia. *New York Times Magazine.*

Toffler, A. (1980). *The third wave.* New York: Bantam.

Toffler, A., & Toffler, H. (1994). *Creating a new civilization.* Atlanta, GA: Turner.

Waldrop, M. H. (1992). *Complexity: The emerging science at the edge of order and chaos.* New York: Simon & Schuster.

Ward, M. (1995). Butterflies and bifurcations: Can chaos theory contribute to our understanding of family systems? *Journal of Marriage and the Family, 57*(3), 629-638.

Watzlawick, P., Weakland, J., & Fisch, M. D. (1974). *Change: Principles of problem formation and problem resolution.* New York: Norton.

Watts, A. G. (1996). Toward a policy for lifelong career development: A transatlantic perspective. *Career Development Quarterly, 45,* 41-53.

Wegman, R. G. (1991). From job to job. *Journal of Employment Counseling 28,* 8-12.

Wegman, R. G., Chapman, R., & Johnson, M. (1995). *Looking for work in the neweconomy.* Salt Lake City, UT: Olympus.

Weiss, D. J., Dawis, R. V., England, G. W., & Lofquist, L. H. (1967). *Manual for the Minnesota Satisfaction Questionnaire.* Minneapolis, MN: University of Minnesota.

CHAPTER 4

CAREER COUNSELING
1990 TO PRESENT

Nancy L. Crumpton

This chapter examines recent developments in career theory and career development interventions from 1990 to the present. Gender, multicultural, and gay and lesbian issues are also explored as they relate to career development.

Existing career development theories have been revisited, evaluated, updated and broadened in the past decade and several new concepts have been introduced. Where new theories and applications flourished in the 1980s, the decade that followed has seen significant economic, social and cultural factors challenge the established theoretical base. Theoretical concepts of vocational choice and vocational adjustment have become more complicated with factors of racial/ethnic diversity, gender, sexual orientation, socioeconomic influences, and the aging work force. Sharf (2002) has categorized career development theories by trait-factor type (Dawis & Lofquist, 1984; Holland, 1997), lifespan theories (Ginzberg, Ginsburg, Axelrad, & Herma, 1951; Gottfredson, 1981, 1996; Super, 1957, 1990), constructivist approaches (Neimeyer, 1992; Savickas, 1997; Young, Valach, & Collin, 1996), social learning (Krumboltz, 1996), career decision-making approach (Tiedeman, 1979; Tiedeman, Miller, & Tied-

Issues in Career Development, 81–99
Copyright © 2005 by Information Age Publishing
All rights of reproduction in any form reserved.

man, 1990), social cognitive (Hackett & Betz, 1981) and family focus/parental influence (Roe & Lunneborg, 1990). A concept referenced in the 1990s was the connection between career counseling and personal counseling in terms of the prominence of personal issues that are a part of career counseling and vice versa. Personal identity, whether it is relative to gender, ethnic or racial affiliation, social status, sexual orientation or age is a significant component of an individual's career development (Croteau & Thiel, 1993; Davidson & Gilbert, 1993; Krumboltz, 1993).

Career development has been expanded from a cognitive information processing perspective by Peterson, Sampson, and Reardon (1991); Peterson, Sampson, Reardon, and Lenz, 1996; Sampson, Lenz, Reardon, and Peterson (1999); and Sampson, Peterson, Reardon, and Lenz (2000). According to the authors, this approach to delivering career counseling has been evolving since 1971 at Florida State University, Center for the Study of Technology in Counseling and Career Development. Career problem solving within this theoretical context is primarily a cognitive process where the client is involved in problem solving activities that increase information-processing skills to be able to make career decisions. Concepts in the cognitive information processing theory include the 10 basic assumptions which provide procedures for incorporating decision-making skills to facilitate the growth of information-processing skills and enhance the client's ability to become a career problem solver.

Zunker (2002) presents their model of the cognitive information processing theory, giving a clearer picture of the concept's application to career counseling. The acronym CASVE, which covers the domain of decision making, consists of communication, analysis, synthesis, valuing, and execution includes the stages of problem perception, evaluation and solution within the counseling framework. Furthermore, Zunker (2002) posits that "Counselors assist clients in identifying actions and elements of actions that provide clues to solving problems" (p. 139).

By 1990, Holland's theory was the dominant work in career research. An annotated bibliography by Holland and G. Gottfredson lists more than 400 studies related to aspects of the theory (Osipow & Fitzgerald, 1996). Throughout the past decade, Holland's (1992) theory has been extensively studied in terms of the validity of the personality types and environment congruence (Niles, 1993; Thompson, Flynn, & Griffith, 1994) as well as interest congruence (Brown & Gore, 1994). There have been studies to correlate Holland's (1992) RIASEC types to personality types or variables measured by other personality inventories such as the NEO Personality Inventory (Costa & McCrae, 1989), NEO Five-Factor Model (Hogan & Blake, 1999; Tokar & Fischer, 1998; Tokar, Fischer, & Subich, 1998; and Tokar & Swanson, 1995), Millon's (1983) personality styles (Strack, 1994), and the Personality Styles Inventory (Silver & Malone, 1993). These studies have attempted to conceptualize the constructs in Holland's theory to measures that could also be used to identify vocational behavior. Vocational identity continues to be a primary focus of research (Osipow, 1999). Relating vocational identity to career indecision (Conneran & Hartman, 1993) has provided valuable information to career counselors. Extending these studies to inner-city high school students, Landany, Melincoff, Constantine, and Love (1997) determined commitment level to career choices was related to vocational identity.

Application of Holland's concept of congruence to women and culturally diverse persons has also flourished in the past decade. Understanding the interpretation of personality types as they relate to women has been investigated by Holland (1997). He found higher scores on realistic, investigative and enterprising scales for men and higher social, artistic, and conventional scales for women. Self-efficacy showed little difference between men and women based on the Holland types (Betz, Harmon, & Borgen, 1996; Betz, Borgen, Kaplan, & Harmon, 1998).

Within the United States, studies have examined the fit of Holland's hexagon model to interests of Caucasians, African Americans, Asian Americans, Native Americans and Hispanic Americans (Day, Rounds, & Swaney, 1998). These authors concluded the model was adequate for these populations. However, to Sharf (2002), "Information about the appropriateness of Holland's typological system for specific cultural groups is neither sufficient nor consistent enough to allow generalizations about its usefulness for specific groups" (p. 114). Holland's model has been used to measure occupational interest in many countries, including China, Israel, Australia, France, Nigeria and New Zealand (Sharf, 2002). The Self-Directed Search-Australian version was reviewed in the *Mental Measurements Yearbook, Fifteenth Edition* (Crumpton, 2003). Studies that measured usefulness of Holland's typology in other countries have indicated less applicability in variables of congruence, interests and job satisfaction, but provide useful information for career counselors and researchers (Farh, Leong, & Law, 1998; Leong, Austin, Sekaran, & Komarraju, 1998).

Life-span theory, as described by Donald Super (1990) and his colleagues, continues to be redefined. His life-career rainbow and archway of career determinants explains how individuals see themselves and their situations as determined by their personality characteristics, values, needs, interests, intelligence, aptitudes and special abilities. Self-concept continually develops as individuals interact with community, school, family, and peers in the context of their society. This development creates changes in roles and values during the life span. Learning more about career development during an individual's lifetime, as well as defining self concept, has been the focus of research in the last decade (Bandura, 1997; Bejian

& Salomone, 1995; Betz, 1994; and Herr, 1997). Stead and Watson (1994) indicate that the Archway Model (Super, 1990) gives evidence of "the interaction of situational, historical, socio-economic, psychological and biological determinants in the career-shaping process" (p. 234).

According to Osipow and Fitzgerald (1996), Super's theory is applicable to both personal and vocational counseling. As a result of its structure, Super's theory offers "moderately specific guidelines for the practice of counseling ... to try to appraise the life stage of a client in order to define relevant counseling goals" (p. 143). By using vocational assessment, experiences in everyday life, community resources and occupational exploration, the client can be assisted in clarifying the self-concept within the context of the life stage. This information would be the determinants of a decision-making sequence in counseling (Osipow & Fitzgerald, 1996).

Application of life stage theories to women has been investigated and the appropriateness of the stage issues has been challenged due to the differences in the life experiences of women (Lippert, 1997; Ornstein & Isabella, 1990). Cultural differences in application of stage theories have also been recently studied as related to Native Americans (McCormick & Amundson, 1997) and African Americans (Cheatham, 1990). Sharf (2002) has included discussion of the minority identity development model (Atkinson, Morten, & Sue, 1998) to assist in conceptualizing Super's theory to minority populations.

Gottfredson's (1996) theory of career development, which also follows a developmental interpretation, has more recent definitions of circumscription and compromise as significant components of her theory. Circumscription deals with factors that come into play to limit career choices throughout the life span. Gender influences and the perceived level of prestige associated with a particular occupation will limit the categories of occupations that are acceptable. Helwig (1998) studied second-, fourth- and sixth-graders and found that they chose occupations highly valued by society in upper grades. This finding is supportive of Gottfredson's theory indicating prestige influences career preferences at age nine and older (Gottfredson, 1981, 1996).

An individual's situation can be influenced by environmental factors such as the labor market and career preparation that limit career choice. An individual may have to modify his or her choices to alternatives that compromise the initial choices. According to Gottfredson's theory, these compromises are made based on the following order: interest first, prestige second, and gender type last. Other researchers have identified the influence of interest areas on compromise (Hall, Kelly, & Van Buren, 1995) as well as differences in culturally diverse populations (Leong & Chou, 1994; Leung, 1993). Studies have resulted in differing orders of compromise. An important contribution of the developmental or life-span theories of career development has been to identify the impact of gender-role stereotyping in career exploration and the need for elementary school children to receive occupational information that does not reinforce gender-role stereotypes (Sharf, 2002).

Work adjustment theory has also seen revision during the past decade (Dawis & Lofquist, 1984). Work adjustment theory has also been applied to predicted work adjustment based on 18 propositions and corollaries that define the relationship between person-environment fit, job satisfaction and tenure. Satisfaction with the occupation selected by an individual and his/her satisfactoriness to the employer exist when there is fit between the individual and the job. Values, abilities, personality styles and interests define the theory. To better represent the interaction of the individual with the environment Lofquist and Dawis (1991) added the term person-environment-correspondence (PEC). The validity of work adjustment theory or PEC has been supported by over 250 studies (Sharf, 2002). Research has demonstrated that work adjustment theory is useful in understanding the person-environment fit between individuals and jobs as well as individuals and organizations (Bretz & Judge, 1994). Because of the changing labor market, the need may exist to identify worker satisfaction in a market where workers may be in several jobs, rather than one job. Dawis (1996) presented definitions of personality structure, personality style, abilities, values and environmental structure to be able to more clearly apply the PEC model. The current theory (Dawis, 2000) has also been applied to gifted adolescents to better understand their educational and vocational choices (Benbow & Lubinski, 1997; Lubinski & Benbow, 2000).

Lent, Brown, and Hackett (1994) have researched interacting influences among individuals, their behaviors and environments based on Bandura's (1986) triadic reciprocal model of causality termed social cognitive career theory (SCCT). This theory is an effort to conceptually link and integrate existing career development theories from a social cognitive perspective. "SCCT highlights three intricately linked variables through which individuals help to regulate their own career behavior: self-efficacy beliefs, outcome expectations, and personal goals" (p. 312).

Self-efficacy beliefs are how persons judge their own abilities to perform tasks. Beliefs are determined by a person's performance, vicarious learning, social persuasion and physiology in different situations. Success in particular areas will increase the self-efficacy belief, whereas failure will diminish the belief. Outcome expectations are what people believe will happen as a result of certain behaviors. In terms of career direction, outcome beliefs are determined by actual perceptions of outcomes as well as information that is obtained through observation or information received through another's experiences (Bandura, 1997; Lent, Brown, & Hackett, 1996).

According to Lent and Brown (1996) personal goals are affected by an individual's self-efficacy and outcome expectations and are determined by what the individual believes in those areas. When positive outcomes are expected, goals are usually formulated that will maintain participation in the activity or increase involvement. A feedback loop is formed depending on the success or failure in an activity and a pattern is developed. Lent and Brown (1996) state that this process is repeated throughout the life span and becomes stable in adulthood. Persons who have had limited experiences to obtain occupational self-efficacy and outcome expectations tend to have restricted interests. Abilities and values can also impact self-efficacy and outcome expectations. The entire process is affected by the context in which the person functions such as gender, race/ethnicity, socioeconomic status and inherited traits. Gender and race components are attributed to differences in learning opportunities and experiences (Lent & Brown, 1996).

Although the individual has choices, the context in which those choices are made influence goal setting in relation to the individual's self-efficacy, outcome expectations and interests. SCCT also states that opportunity has an impact on career direction. The ability of a person to persevere and achieve in work tasks are areas of concern to SCCT and are impacted by the level of self-efficacy and the positive or negative outcome belief of the individual. This analysis of performance behavior can provide opportunity for individuals to evaluate their efficacy beliefs and direct efforts toward intervention (Bandura, 1997).

A recent focus of career development theories is the concept of contextualism. This explanation of career development is based on contructivism that was derived in part from personal construct theory. George A. Kelly's (1955) personal construct theory of personality was very different from other approaches at that time. Kelly proposed that individuals interpret and organize the events and social relationships that are a part of their lives in a pattern and predictions about the individual and social contacts and events are based on this pattern. Individuals use this understanding of their own and others' behaviors to guide their own behavior and predict the behavior of others (Schultz & Schultz, 2001). Construct is an intellectual hypothesis that people devise and use to understand events in their lives. According to Kelly (1955) constructs that are dichotomous, limited or broad, can be revised (constructive alternativism), individualized, tested in experience, and repeatedly follow a pattern.

Sharf (2002) stated that constructivism is a philosophical position developed from postmodernism. Within this position individuals construct their own reality depending on the way they perceive and interpret events and relationships in their lives. In the area of vocational constructs, persons "find a purpose in work, control how they work, evaluate the choices they make and the work they do, and develop a sense of identity through work" (p. 281). Collin (1997) offers criticism of the more traditional theories of career development and suggests that they are not broad enough in conceptualizing the environment of an individual. She indicates that the meaning of career is determined by the perspective and purposes of the individual and may not be a universal view. Approaches recently developed that are consistent with contextualism include action theory (Young & Valach, 1996) and hermeneutical inquiry (Young & Collin, 1992).

Action theory most simply defined is the total action by all persons involved in an activity with focus on the context in which the activity occurs. The entirety of the event is observed as well as the context within which interaction occurs and the changes that result from that interaction (Young, Valach, & Collin, 1996). Joint actions are those that occur between people and an individual's career constructs (values, interests, work identity, and behaviors) and develops through interaction. As career is defined by this theory, the actions occur over a period of time, become complex and derive social meaning from the actions by connecting constructs, evaluating plans and goals as well as internal thought processes (Zunker, 2002).

Cabral and Salamone (1990) have also brought to consideration the role that chance plays in career development. They represent that most models of career decision making are based on behavior patterns that are typical and do not take into account the role that unforeseen events play in the process. They propose a model of career decision making that would take into consideration the chance influences as well as those considered normative. The effect of chance on career decisions is considered inevitable, playing an important role, dependent on the stage of development of the individual and the context in which the events occur. These authors support a contextual approach to career counseling in which the individual is able to learn from past actions and identify or build skills to successfully meet the effects of chance events.

Another recent development in career counseling theory is consideration of converging career development theories to be able to more directly utilize theory in counseling practice (Savickas, 1995; Sharf, 1996). The conflicts in operational definitions between career counseling, psychotherapy and career development theory have created difficulty in integrating research efforts (Zunker, 2002). As indicated in Zunker's text, at the meeting of a special interest group of the Counseling Psychology Division of the American Psychological Association in 1992, the convergence of career theories was not recommended, although clarification of the varying constructs of the theories was considered a useful effort. Contextualism will continue to be included in research to better define the individual and the environment of career development (Savickas, 1995). The issues addressed by a contextual approach may offer a way to provide answers to the questions posed by those considering a more convergent view of career development and counseling.

Gay/Lesbian Issues

Career counseling literature related to gay/lesbian issues has presented concerns that deal with the ethical provision of career counseling services to this population as well as required training of counselors to be able to understand career development theory in the context of gay and lesbian individuals (Buhrke & Douce, 1991). Integrating sexual orientation in career counseling has not been explored in the literature to a great extent until recently (Croteau & Theil, 1993; Hetherington, 1991). The dynamics of integrating personal identity and vocational concerns in the career counseling process have been identified as "(a) signaling lesbian and gay affirmation in career counseling practice, (b) enhancing the development of a positive gay or lesbian identity in the context of career development work, and (c) recognizing and integrating the reality of antigay stigma in career counseling" (Croteau & Theil, 1993, p. 174).

According to Croteau and Theil (1993) career counselors are able to show clients their understanding and support of gay and lesbian concerns by the ways they perform work on a daily basis. Counselors are able to use language both written and spoken that is inclusive of different sexual orientations as well as displaying items in offices that present an interest and affirmation of gay and lesbian issues such as posters, journals or other materials. Other examples included wording forms in a way in which categories would not exclude gay and lesbian lifestyle situations and providing the option to clients of working with a gay or lesbian counselor (Committee on Lesbian and Gay Concerns, American Psychological Association, 1991; Eldridge & Barnett, 1991).

Acknowledging the existence of the stigma that is in place in many work places is another way in which counselors are able to more effectively address career counseling issues. The counseling process is made more effective by exploring the impact of antigay attitudes both in the workplace and as a personal concern of the client (Belz, 1993; Croteau & Theil, 1993). The counselor can provide techniques and practice in evaluating work environments, identify resources that provide information about nondiscrimination statements by corporations indicating a more supportive environment, and assist in developing networks of individuals within the gay and lesbian community (Croteau & Hedstrom, 1993; Schmitz, 1988).

Testing is considered an important tool for self-assessment in terms of values clarification and understanding of the impact of external pressures on the individual apart from his/her actual interests. Current testing materials available to assist in career decision making do not take into account the dynamics particular to conflicts for sexual minority groups due to potential job discrimination. Results of testing may indicate career indecision, when in fact fear of an oppressive work environment due to sexual orientation is the only factor contributing to the indecision (Chung, 1995; Croteau & Hedstrom, 1993). The counselor should also have information to share with the client regarding community and national gay/lesbian networks that would provide contact persons and support (Belz, 1993).

Theoretical applications of Astin (1984), Farmer (1985) and Gottfredson (1981) have been considered in understanding the vocational behavior of gay, lesbian and bisexual individuals (Morgan & Brown, 1991). According to Chung (1995), "Farmer's model seems to be the most promising because of its comprehensiveness, operationalizability and testability" (p. 178). Career development approaches that take into account environmental and personal factors are needed to provide counseling that is appropriate. According to Chung personal factors that have been identified include career interests, values, socioeconomic status, career aspirations, and skills. Environmental factors incorporate not only labor market information but also barriers that exist to gay, lesbian and bisexual individuals. These barriers may include discrimination, stereotyping individuals in certain occupations by identifying particular occupations inappropriate for gay or lesbian persons, prejudice and stigma as a result of sexual orientation and the fear of AIDS (Chung, 1995). Investigation of the interaction of the personal and environmental factors is encouraged to provide a better understanding of the career decision making process of gay, lesbian and bisexual individuals.

Croteau and Hedstrom (1993) discussed the role of the counselor in determining client perception and counseling intervention as a result of that perception. There is a concern that counselors understand gay and lesbian clients in the ways they are similar to heterosexual clients and in the ways they are different as a result of sexual orientation in the area of career development. John E. Elliot (1993) presented career development issues for gay and lesbian clients as a nonethnic cultural minority that have a specific history, culture, jargon, ethical behavior, and community. He addressed issues of discrimination that develop as a result of individuals who decide to be open on the job about their sexual orientation and the need for counselors to be culturally skilled in working with this popu-

lation. Counselor educators were challenged to provide training in awareness of the jargon, of the intricacies of gay and lesbian issues and to offer
experiences in practicum with gay and lesbian clients or counseling professionals. Counselors need to be familiar with the climate of their own
communities in regard to personnel policies and opinions of employers in
hiring lesbian and gay persons.

Ruth E. Fassinger (1995) addressed the issues of lesbians in applying
existing career development theory. Her discussion of negative self concept, stigma of sexual orientation, occupational discrimination, stereotyping, lack of role models, and bias in testing and counseling present
significant challenges in career decision making. Interesting in her review
was empirical information stating that two thirds of lesbians have not
shared their sexual identity with employers, only one third have told
coworkers and over one third have not informed anyone (Eldridge & Gilbert, 1990; Fassinger, 1991). Concerns related to this behavior involve a
fear of job loss or loss of income (60%-75% of women) as well as the discrimination and hostility in the work place associated with disclosure
(Morgan & Brown, 1991). From Fassinger's perspective, valid and reliable
measures of identity development of lesbian women who are demograph-
ically diverse should be developed. These could be used in conjunction
with existing measures to determine the extent current theories of vocational development are appropriately applicable to lesbians (Fassinger,
1995). Without these empirical studies to extend existing theory to sexual
minority individuals, career counseling theory will lose relevance and
counseling practice will not be efficacious with this population (Fassinger,
1991; Fitzgerald & Betz, 1994).

Other areas of competence required of counselors include disclosure
management strategies (Gonsiorek, 1993), explicit information and skill
workshops to address ways to include lesbian/gay activities in an interview
or resume, and networking within gay and lesbian organizations (Elliot,
1993). Also addressed are problem-solving strategies for coupling and
parenting (Browning, Reynolds, & Dworkin, 1991). Again, research in the
1990s directs the reader to extend empirical research in career development theory and test development to be inclusive of the specific characteristics and areas of concern to the gay and lesbian population.

Gender and Racial-Ethnic Issues

According to Cheatham (1990) much of the career development theory
that has been presented through the years has been based on Eurocentric
characteristics and concepts, and as a result there is a discrepancy in the
applicability of these theories to African Americans. Similar statements

are made in the literature relative to Asian Americans (Leong, 1993; Yang, 1991), Hispanic Americans (Bowman, 1993; Hawks & Muha, 1991), and Native Americans (Martin, 1991). Gender differences in career development and planning have also been addressed in relation to life-style opportunities and demands in the context of the lives of women and men (Cook, 1993). The research challenges the general application of existing theoretical approaches in career counseling and the need to specifically address the differences in educating future counselors.

Literature relevant to the career development of Native Americans is limited. According to Martin (1991), 46% of the approximate 1.4 million Native Americans live in the United States either on reservations or other identified Indian areas or in nonmetropolitan locations. His article addressed this population and provided useful information to career counselors working with the Native American population in terms of specific ethnic values and concepts that should direct the career counseling process. Conclusions drawn from his research indicated that the counselor needed to understand the client's family structure and the influence of family networks as the importance of this influence directs the client's vocational decision making. Studies were reviewed that also cautioned the use of psychological testing with the Native American population as cultural influences could affect their usefulness as a career counseling tool. When standardized testing is determined inappropriate due to cultural factors, the use of situational assessments, work samples or on-the-job evaluations are better strategies for assessment.

Of interest also was the discussion of the error in assuming the Native American client is part of a homogeneous group. There is a general insight into cultural factors that influence the career development process, but there is considerable difference within and between tribes as well as whether the client lives in a rural or urban location (Martin, 1991). According to Zunker (2002) career counselors will need to be sensitive to the value orientation of Native Americans. "The challenge for counselors is to assist Native Americans in preserving the positive aspects of their heritage while encouraging them to modify some behaviors" (Zunker, 2002, p. 288).

Leong (1993) discussed the process of career counseling for Asian American clients as related to the complex styles of interpersonal communication and the conflict that occurs in the communication process when the indirect, guarded and subtle style of Asian Americans is misunderstood by the career counselor. He stresses the importance of personal honor and avoiding loss of face in the development of their communication style. Lynch and Hanson (1992) describe the way information is transmitted through contextual cues in Asian culture more than by explicit conversation. There also can be misunderstanding of the direction of counseling when the Asian American client is identifying the counselor as the expert or authority figure. The counselor would need to provide a structured approach to meet expectations of the client. Without this, the client may terminate the counseling process because he or she considers it ineffective or more negatively, considers the experience a harmful one (Leong, 1991). As a result of this valuation, the counseling process may take longer to establish, with progress being more gradual (Leong, 1993).

Differences in socialization between Asian Americans and Caucasian Americans present another area of concern to the career counselor. The individualistic nature of Caucasian Americans promotes self-actualization, self-concept and assertiveness that are cornerstones of many of the career development theories. Individuals are respected in Western culture for their independence and autonomy. Applying these values and approaches of self-actualization to a culture that is more collectivistic and extrinsic would not be effective (Leong, 1991). In Asian culture respect is gained through the individual's responsibility to a social group and self-interest is less important than the needs of the group (Zunker, 2002). Asian women have an additional conflict in terms of their view of freedom of choice in the context of a traditional, well-defined gender role within the family and community. In her study of Chinese American women, Cook (1993) addressed the problems in applying career counseling interventions for women in general to Chinese American women because of the conflicts in value orientation.

Bowman (1993) reported limited literature available for the study of Hispanic Americans utilizing career counseling. General characteristics defined Hispanic families as patriarchal, with well-defined gender roles, intense loyalty and respect for family (Sue & Sue, 1990). According to Ivey and Ivey (1999) as cited in Zunker (2002), the particular Hispanic descent is an important distinction for Mexican Americans, Cuban Americans and Puerto Rican Americans. There is a range of the level of acculturation and socioeconomic backgrounds among Hispanic persons as well as variance in value systems which make a difference to the application of career development theory (Zunker, 2002).

In 1990, Cheatham addressed the career counseling needs of African American clients being met within the framework of Africentrism. According to this theory, African Americans have evolved from a legacy of slavery determining "enforced isolation and disenfranchisement" (p. 337). Their socialization, determinant norms, role definition and group identification has been characterized by their heritage of slavery. There is minimal emphasis on the individual and identification is defined by the reference of family, friends and community. Cheatham emphasizes the importance of this heritage and legacy for African Americans in consideration of cultural differences in career development. He notes the importance of recognizing these cultural references in comparison to Eurocentrism, inherent in most career development theories. Cheatham (1990) states that the existing theories do not consider the African American's experience with racial discrimination, their perceptions of the meaning of work, availability of counseling for career guidance or the components of the labor market that have a direct influence for career opportunities for African Americans. He recommends the shift from an etic perspective to an emic, culturally specific perspective, considering the impact of heritage within the Eurocentric components of career development theory.

The contribution of gender differences to the interpretation of career counseling theories has been addressed by Cook (1993). Gender socialized differences of achievement, relationships, and work values are shaped by the interaction of men and women with their environments. Internally and externally there is a difference in how men and women assess quality of relationships, self worth, and commitment to career, power, and home and career responsibilities. Cook states, "On a daily basis, individuals bring certain behavioral predispositions to situations, and environments present individuals with certain opportunities, expectations, demands, and rewards based on their biological sex" (p. 227). Because the worlds of men and women are defined differently, career counseling must take into account both the individual differences and environmental differences of the person. Socioemotional factors in combining home and career are issues for both genders and life patterns become more complicated in dual career-families. Employer and spousal expectations in both traditional and nontraditional family structures present career challenges. Cook's discussion of the implications of these concepts to career counselors addresses consideration of relationship and family characteristics as well as occupational goals when assisting in career plans, taking the gendered context of the work environment into consideration, and the evaluation of the counselor's own gender bias in the career counseling process.

Many issues define this past decade in terms of the direction of theoretical analysis in career development. Existing theories have extended their applications to be more consistent with current social, cultural and occupational environments. Throughout the research, themes of contextualism are prevalent and this concept will contribute to interesting study. Deliberate considerations of racial/ethnic and cultural diversity, gender, and sexual orientation are considered imperative in ethical, comprehensive career counseling practice. More research is needed to competently apply career development theory in areas of ethnic and cultural diversity. These issues are also directly applicable to counseling education programs in preparing counselors to meet challenges of career counseling in the future.

REFERENCES

Astin, H. S. (1984). The meaning of work in women's lives: A sociopsychological model of career choice and work behavior. *The Counseling Psychologist, 12,* 117-128.

Atkinson, D. R., Morten, G., & Sue, D. W. (1998). *Counseling American minorities: A cross-cultural perspective* (5th ed.). New York: McGraw-Hill.

Bandura, A. (1986). *Social foundations of thought and action: A social cognitive theory.* Englewood Cliffs, NJ: Prentice-Hall.

Bandura, A. (1997). *Self-efficacy: The exercise of control.* San Francisco: W. H. Freeman.

Bejian, D. V., & Salomone, P. R. (1995). Understanding midlife career renewal: Implications for counseling. *Career Development Quarterly, 44,* 52-63.

Belz, J. R. (1993). Sexual orientation as a factor in career development. *Career Development Quarterly, 41,* 197-200.

Benbow, C. P., & Lubinski, D. (1997). Intellectually talented children: How can we best meet their needs? In N. Colangelo & G. A. Davis (Eds.), *Handbook of gifted education* (2nd ed., pp. 155-169). Boston: Allyn & Bacon.

Betz, N. E. (1994). Self concept theory in career development and counseling. *Career Development Quarterly, 43,* 32-42.

Betz, N., Harmon, L., & Borgen, F. H. (1996). The relationships of self-efficacy for the Holland themes to gender, occupational group membership, and vocational interests. *Journal of Counseling Psychology, 43,* 90-93.

Bowman, S. L. (1993). Career intervention strategies for ethnic minorities. *Career Development Quarterly, 42,* 14-26.

Bretz, R. D., Jr., & Judge, T. A. (1994). Person-organization fit and the theory of work adjustment. Implications for satisfaction, tenure, and career success. *Journal of Vocational Behavior, 44,* 32-54.

Brown, S. D., & Gore, P. A., Jr. (1994). An evaluation of interest congruence indices: Distribution characteristics and measurement properties. *Journal of Vocational Behavior, 45,* 310-327.

Browning, C., Reynolds, A., & Dworkin, S. (1991) Affirmative psychotherapy for lesbian women. *The Counseling Psychologist, 19,* 177-196.

Brown, S. D., & Gore, P. A., Jr. (1994). An evaluation of interest congruence indices: Distribution characteristics and measurement properties. *Journal of Vocational Behavior, 45,* 310-327.

Buhrke, R. B., & Douce, L. A. (1991). Training issues for counseling psychologists in working with lesbian women and gay men. *The Counseling Psychologist, 19,* 216-234.

Cabral, A. C., & Salomone, P. R. (1990). Chance and careers: Normative versus contextual development. *Career Development Quarterly, 39,* 5-17.

Cheatham, H. E. (1990). Africentricity and career development of African Americans. *Career Development Quarterly, 38,* 334-346.

Chung, Y. B. (1995). Career decision making of lesbian, gay, and bisexual individuals. *Career Development Quarterly, 44,* 178-191.

Collin, A. (1997). Career in context. *British Journal of Guidance & Counseling, 25,* 435-447.

Committee on Lesbian and Gay Concerns, American Psychological Association. (1991). Avoiding heterosexual bias in language. *American Psychologist, 46,* 973-974.

Conneran, J. M., & Hartman, B. W. (1993). The concurrent validity of the Self-Directed Search in identifying chronic career indecision among vocational education students. *Journal of Career Development, 19,* 197-208.

Cook, E. P. (1993). The gendered context of life: Implications for women's and men's career-life plans. *Career Development Quarterly, 41,* 227-238.

Costa, P. T., Jr., & McCrae, R. R. (1989). *NEOPI/FFI professional manual supplement.* Odessa, FL: Psychological Assessment Resources.

Croteau, J. M., & Hedstrom, S. M. (1993). Integrating commonality and difference: The key to career counseling with lesbian women and gay men. *Career Development Quarterly, 41,* 201-209.

Croteau, J. M., & Theil, M. J. (1993). Integrating sexual orientation in career counseling: Acting to end a form of the personal-career dichotomy. *Career Development Quarterly, 42,* 174-180.

Crumpton, N. L. (2003). Review of the Self-Directed Search, Second Australian Edition. In B. S. Plake, J. C. Impara & R. A. Spies (Eds.), *The fifteenth mental measurements yearbook* (p. 223). Lincoln, NE: Buros Institute of Mental Measurements.

Davidson, S. L., & Gilbert, L. A. (1993). Career counseling is a personal matter. *Career Development Quarterly, 42,* 149-153.

Dawis, R. V. (1996). The theory of work adjustment and person-environment-correspondence counseling. In D. Brown, L. Brooks, & Associates (Eds.), *Career choice and development* (3rd ed., pp. 75-115). San Francisco: Jossey-Bass.

Dawis, R. V. (2000). Work adjustment theory. In A. E. Kazdin (Ed.), Encyclopedia of psychology. New York: Oxford University Press.

Dawis, R. V., & Lofquist, L. H. (1984). *A psychological theory of work adjustment.* Minneapolis, MN: University of Minnesota Press.

Day, S. X., Rounds, J., & Swaney, K. (1998). The structure of vocational interests for diverse racial-ethnic groups. *Psychological Science, 9,* 40-44.

Eldridge, N. S., & Barnett, D. C. (1991). Counseling gay and lesbian students. In V. Wall & N. Evans (Eds.), *Beyond tolerance: Addressing issues facing gay and lesbian students and staff on college campuses.* Washington, DC: ACPA Media Board.

Eldridge, N. S., & Gilbert, L. A. (1990). Correlates of relationship satisfaction in lesbian couples. *Psychology of Women Quarterly, 14,* 43-62.

Elliot, J. E. (1993). Career development with lesbian and gay clients. *Career Development Quarterly, 41,* 210-226.

Farh, J., Leong, F. T. L., & Law, K. (1998). Cross-cultural validity of Holland's model in Hong Kong. *Journal of Vocational Behavior, 52,* 425-440.

Farmer, H. S. (1985). Model of career and achievement motivation for women and men. *Journal of Counseling Psychology, 32,* 363-390.

Fassinger, R. E. (1991). The hidden minority: Issues and challenges in working with lesbian women and gay men. *The Counseling Psychologist, 19,* 157-176.

Fassinger, R. E. (1995). From invisibility to integration: Lesbian identity in the workplace. *Career Development Quarterly, 44,* 148-168.

Fitzgerald, L. F., & Betz, N. E. (1994). Career development in cultural context: The role of gender, race, class, and sexual orientation. In M. Savickas & R. Lent (Eds.), *Convergence in career development theories* (pp. 103-117). Palo Alto, CA: Consulting Psychologist Press.

Ginzberg, E., Ginsburg, S. W., Axelrad, S., & Herma, J. L. (1951). *Occupational choice: An approach to a general theory.* New York: Columbia University Press.

Gottfredson, L. S. (1981). Circumscription and compromise: A developmental theory of occupational aspirations. *Journal of Counseling Psychology, 28,* 545-579.

Gottfredson, L. S. (1996). A theory of circumscription and compromise. In D. Brown & L. Brooks (Eds.), *Career choice and development: Applying contemporary theories to practice* (3rd ed., pp. 179-232). San Francisco: Josey-Bass.

Gonsiorek, C. J. (1993). Threat, stress, and adjustment: Mental health and the workplace for gay and lesbian individuals. In L. Diamant (Ed.), *Homosexual issues in the workplace* (pp. 243-264). New York: Wiley.

Hackett, G., & Betz, N. E. (1981). A self-efficacy approach to the career development of women. *Journal of Vocational Behavior, 18,* 326-339.

Hall, A. S., Kelly, K. R., & Van Buren, J. B. (1995). Effects of grade level, community of residence, and sex on adolescent career interests in the zone of acceptablealternatives. *Journal of Career Develoment, 21,* 223-232.

Hawks, B. K., & Muha, D. (1991). Facilitating the career development of minorities: Doing it differently this time. *Career Development Quarterly, 39,* 251-262.

Helwig, A. A. (1998). Gender-role stereotyping: Testing theory with a longitudinal sample. *Sex Roles, 38,* 402-423.

Herr, E. L. (1997). Super's life-span, life-space approach and its outlook for refinement. *Career Development Quarterly, 45,* 238-246.

Hetherington, C. (1991). Life planning and career counseling with gay and lesbian students. In N. J. Evans & V. A. Wall (Eds.), *Beyond tolerance: Gays, lesbians and bisexuals on campus* (pp. 131-146). Alexandria, VA: American College Personnel Association.

Hogan, R., & Blake, R. (1999). John Holland's vocational typology and personality theory. *Journal of Vocational Behavior, 55,* 41-56.

Holland, J. L. (1992). *Making vocational choices: A theory of personalities and work environments* (2nd ed.). Odessa, FL: Psychological Assessment Resources.

Holland, J. L. (1997). *Making vocational choices: A theory of vocational personalities and work environments* (3rd ed.). Odessa FL: Psychological Assessment Resources.

Ivey, A. E., & Ivey, M. B. (1999). *Intentional interviewing & counseling* (4th ed.). Pacific Grove, CA: Brooks/Cole.

Kelly, G. A. (1955). *The psychology of personal constructs.* New York: Norton.

Krumboltz, J. D. (1993). Integrating career and personal counseling. *Career Development Quarterly, 42,* 143-148.

Krumboltz, J. D. (1996). A learning theory of career counseling. In M. L. Savickas & W. B. Walsh (Eds.), *Handbook of career counseling theory and practice* (pp. 55-80). Palo Alto, CA: Consulting Psychologists Press.

Landany, N., Melincoff, D. S., Constantine, M. G., & Love, R. (1997). At-risk urban high school students' commitment to career choices. *Journal of Counseling and Development, 76,* 45-52.

Lent, R. W., & Brown, S. D. (1996). Social cognitive approach to career development: An overview. *Career Development Quarterly, 44,* 310-321.

Lent, R. W., Brown, S. D., & Hackett, G. (1994). Toward a unifying social cognitive theory of career and academic interest, choice, and performance [Monograph]. *Journal of Vocational Behavior, 45,* 79-122.

Lent, R. W., Brown, S. D., & Hackett, G. (1996). Career development from a social cognitive perspective. In D. Brown, L. Brooks, & Associates (Eds.), *Career choice and development* (3rd ed., pp. 373-421). San Francisco: Jossey-Bass.

Leong, F. T L. (1991). Career development attributes and occupational values of Asian American and white American college students. *Career Development Quarterly, 39,* 273-383.

Leong, F. T. L. (1993). The career counseling process with racial-ethnic minorities: The case of Asian Americans. *Career Development Quarterly, 42,* 26-41.

Leong, F. T. L., Austin, J. T., Sekaran, U., & Knomarraju, M. (1998). An evaluation of the cross-cultural validity of Holland's theory: Career choices by workers in India. *Journal of Vocational Behavior, 52,* 441-455.

Leong, F. T. L., & Chou, E. L. (1994). The role of ethnic identity and acculturation in the vocational behavior of Asian Americans: An integrative review. *Journal of Vocational Behavior, 44,* 155-172.

Leung, S. A. (1993). Circumscription and compromise: A replication study with Asian Americans. *Journal of Counseling Psychology, 40,* 188-193.

Lippert, L. (1997). Women at midlife: Implications for theories of women's adult development. *Journal of Counseling & Development, 76,* 16-22.

Lofquist, L. H., & Dawis, R. V. (1991*). Essentials of person-environment-correspondence counseling*. Minneapolis; MN: University of Minnesota Press.

Lubinski, D., & Benbow, C. P. (2000). States of excellence. *American Psychologist, 53,* 1-14.

Lynch, E. W., & Hanson, M. J. (1992*). Developing cross-cultural competence: A guide for working with young children and their families*. Baltimore: Paul Brookes.

Martin, W. E., Jr. (1991). Career development and American Indians living on reservations: Cross-cultural factors to consider. *Career Development Quarterly, 39,* 273-285.

McCormick, R. M., & Amundson, N. E. (1997). A career-life planning model for First Nations people. *Journal of Employment Counseling, 34,* 171-179.

Miller-Tiedeman, A. L., & Tiedeman, D. V. (1990). Career decision making: An individualistic perspective. In D. Brown, L. Brooks, & Associates. (Eds.), *Career choice and development: Applying contemporary theories to practice* (2nd ed., pp. 308-337). San Francisco: Jossey-Bass.

Millon, T. (1983). The DSM-III: An insider's perspective. *American Psychologist, 38,* 804-814.

Lippert, L. (1997). Women at midlife: Implications for theories of women's adult development. *Journal of Counseling and Development, 76,* 16-22.

Morgan, K. S., & Brown, L. S. (1991). Lesbian career development, work behavior and vocational counseling. *The Counseling Psychologist, 19,* 273-291.

Neimeyer, G. J. (1992). Personal constructs in career counseling and development. *Journal of Career Development, 18,* 163-174.

Niles, S. G. (1993). The relationship between Holland types preferences for career counseling. *Journal of Career Development, 19,* 209-220.

Ornstein, S., & Isabella, L. (1990). Age vs. stage models of career attitudes of women: A partial replication and extension. *Journal of Vocational Behavior, 36,* 1-19.

Osipow, S. H. (1999). Assessing career indecision. *Journal of Vocational Behavior, 55,* 147-154.

Osipow, S. H., & Fitzgerald, L. (1996). *Theories of career development* (4th ed.). Needham Heights, MA: Allyn & Bacon.

Peterson, G. W., Sampson, J. P., Jr., & Reardon, R. C. (1991). *Career development and services: A cognitive approach.* Pacific Grove, CA: Brooks/Cole.

Peterson, G. W., Sampson, J. P., Jr., Reardon, R. C., & Lenz, J. G. (1996). Becoming career problem solvers and decision makers: A cognitive information processing approach. In D. Brown & L. Brooks (Eds.), *Career choice and development* (3rd ed., pp. 423-479). San Francisco: Jossey-Bass.

Roe, A., & Lunneborg, P. W. (1990). Personality development and career choice. In D. Brown & L. Brooks (Eds.), *Career choice and development: Applying contemporary theories to practice* (pp. 68-101). San Francisco: Jossey-Bass.

Sampson, J. P., Jr., Lenz, J. G., Reardon, R. C., & Peterson, G. W. (1999). A cognitive information processing approach to employment problem and decision making. *Career Development Quarterly, 48,* 3-18.

Sampson, J .P., Jr., Peterson, G. W., Reardon, R. C., & Lenz, J. G. (2000). Using readiness assessment to improve career services: A cognitive information processing approach. *Career Development Quarterly, 49,* 146-174.

Savickas, M. L. (1995). Current theoretical issues in vocational psychology: Convergence, divergence, and schism. In W. B. Walsh & S. H. Osipow (Eds.), *Handbook of vocational psychology* (2nd ed., pp. 1-34). Hillsdale, NJ: Erlbaum.

Savickas, M. L. (1997). Constructivist career counseling: Models and methods. *Advances in Personal Construct Psychology, 4,* 149-182.

Schmitz, T. (1988). Career counseling implications with the gay and lesbian population. *Journal of Employment Counseling, 25,* 50-56.

Schultz, D. P., & Schultz, S. E. (2001). *Theories of personality* (7th ed.). Belmont, CA: Wadsworth/Thomson Learning.

Sharf, R. S. (1996). *Theories of psychotherapy and counseling: Concepts and cases.* Pacific Grove, CA: Brooks/Cole.

Sharf, R. S. (2002). *Applying career development theory to counseling* (3rd ed.) Pacific Grove, CA: Brooks/Cole.

Silver, C. B., & Malone, J. E. (1993). A scale of personality styles based on DSM-III-R for investigating occupational choice and leisure activities. *Journal of Career Assessment, 1,* 427-440.

Stead, G. B., & Watson, M. B. (1994). Psychosocial aspects of developmental career theories. Comment on Naicker. *South African Journal of Psychology, 24,* 234-6.

Strack, S. (1994) Relating Millon's personality styles and Holland's occupational types. *Journal of Vocational Behavior, 45,* 41-54.

Sue, D. W., & Sue, D. (1990). *Counseling the culturally different: Theory and practice.* New York: Wiley.

Super, D. E. (1972). Vocational development theory: Persons, positions, and processes. In J. M. Whiteley & A. Resnikoff (Eds.), *Perspectives on vocational development* (pp. 13-33). Washington, DC: American Personnel and Guidance Association.

Super, D. E. (1990). A life-span, life-space approach to career development. In D. Brown, L. Brooks, & Associates (Eds.), *Career choice and development: Applying contemporary theories to practice* (2nd ed., pp. 97-261). San Francisco: Jossey-Bass.

Thompson, J. M., Flynn, R. J., & Griffith, S. A. (1994). Congruence and coherence as predictors of congruent employment outcomes. *Career Development Quarterly, 4,* 271-281.

Tiedeman, D. V., & Miller-Tiedeman, A. L. (1979). Choice and decision processes and career revisited. In A. M. Mitchell, G. B. Jones, & J. D. Krumboltz (Eds.), *Social learning and career decision making* (pp. 160-179). Cranston, RI: Carroll Press.

Tokar, D. M., & Fischer, A. R. (1998). More of RIASEC and the Five-Factor Model of Personality: Direct assessment of Prediger's (1982) and Hogan's (1983) dimensions. *Journal of Vocational Behavior, 52,* 246-259.

Tokar, D. M., Fischer, A. R., & Subich, L. M. (1998). Personality and vocational behavior: A selective review of the literature, 1993-1997. *Journal of Vocational Behavior, 53,* 115-153.

Tokar, D. M., & Swanson, J. L. (1995). Evaluation of the correspondence between Holland's vocational personality typology and the Five-Factor Model of Personality. *Journal of Vocational Behavior, 46,* 89-108.

Yang, J. (1991). Career counseling of Chinese American women: Are they in limbo? *Career Development Quarterly, 39,* 350-360.

Young, R. A., & Collin, A. (1992). *Interpreting career: Hermeneutical studies of lives in context.* Westport, CT: Praeger.

Young, R. A., & Valach, L. (1996). Interpretation and action in career counseling. In M. L. Davickas & W. B. Walsh (Eds.), *Handbook of career counseling theory and practice* (pp. 361-375). Palo Alto, CA: Davies-Black.

Young, R. A., Valach, L., & Collin, A. (1996). A contextual explanation of career. In D. Brown, L. Brooks, & Associates (Eds.), *Career choice and development* (3rd ed., pp. 477-512). San Francisco: Jossey-Bass.

Zunker, V. G. (2002). *Career counseling: applied concepts of life planning* (6th ed., pp. 26-77). Pacific Grove, CA: Brooks/Cole.

CHAPTER 5

A REVIEW OF MODELS OF CAREER INTERVENTIONS

Implications for Career Development

Donald W. Anderson

The new and changing workforce sets the stage for new directions, and demands new interventions in career counseling. The United States has become more diversified, thus creating a need for a varied array of delivering career services. While both older and newer interventions are currently described in the literature, they have had varying degrees of success with diversified populations. It is important that interventions are designed to address the challenges to workers across individual, personal, school, and community levels. This paper addresses career intervention models and strategies, which can be employed by career counselors and others to enhance and address potential barriers to the career development of the changing workforce.

INTRODUCTION

Dramatic changes across cultures in the nature of work, workplace, employer-employee relationships, and career patterns have resulted in

Issues in Career Development, 101–128
Copyright © 2005 by Information Age Publishing
All rights of reproduction in any form reserved.

more complicated career interventions (Kummerow, 2000; Rifkin, 1995). Since Frank Parsons' time, nearly a century of social change has brought forth exciting new models of career development theory and intervention, including new directions for career counseling (Hansen, 2000). We know that career interventions generally have positive effects (Baker & Popowicz, 1983; Spokane & Oliver, 1983). Summaries of the aggregate effects on career knowledge, attitudes, or behaviors demonstrate that career education (Baker & Popowicz, 1983; Hoyt, 1980), career counseling (Holland, Magoon, & Spokane, 1981; Spokane & Oliver, 1983; Oliver & Spokane, 1988), and career guidance (Herr & Cramer, 1996) yield positive results. The literature clearly demonstrates that the utility of such interventions are no longer in doubt (Rounds & Tinsley, 1984). Now we need to determine which interventions work best with which populations and under what circumstances. Consequently, researchers are studying how interventions achieve their effects and how to optimize these effects (Savickas, 1989a). Relatively little research has addressed the outcomes of career counseling processes based on different procedures and conceptual perspectives (McBride, 2001).

To help remedy the nomenclature, definition, and organization problems extant in the field of career development interventions, researchers from the National Research Center for Career and Technical Education (2001) conducted a study (a) to identify a comprehensive list of career development interventions that occur in America's secondary schools, and (b) create taxonomy of the identified interventions. Forty four interventions were identified. The interventions were then rated on five variables (i.e., time, mode, control, place, and size). These ratings were then grouped empirically by means of cluster analysis, producing a four-cluster solution. The four clusters of career development interventions were titled: (a) introductory interventions; (b) advising interventions; (c) curriculum-based interventions; and (d) work-based interventions.

Introductory interventions included career days/fairs, field trips, aptitude assessment, and guidance lessons on personal/social development, career development, and so forth (Wonacott, 2001).

Advising interventions "provide direction, resolve impediments, and sustain planfulness in students about their goals for the future" (Dykeman Ingram, Wood, Charles, Chen, & Herr, 2001, p. 22). This intervention includes academic and career counseling, career-focused individual activities, career peer advising/tutoring, career maturity and interest assessments, college-assisted career guidance, information interviewing, job search preparation, personal/social preparation, portfolios/individual career plans, referral to external training or counseling/assessment, and so forth (Wonacott, 2001).

Curriculum-based interventions include career information and skills infused into curriculum, career/technical education courses, career academic/career magnet schools, school-based enterprises, student clubs/ activities, and tech prep (Dykerman, Ingram, Wood, Charles, & Herr, 2001).

Work based interventions "promote student knowledge and motivation through sustained and meaningful interactions with work sites in the community (Dykeman, Ingram, Wood, Charles, Chen, & Herr, 2001, p. 21). These activities include cooperative education, internships, job shadowing, job coaching, mentoring, service learning/volunteer programs, work study, and youth apprenticeships (Wonacott, 2001).

OLD ASSUMPTIONS AND NEW OBSERVATIONS
CONNECTIONS FROM THE PAST

Career interventions need to address the unique career needs of specific populations, for example, racial and ethnic minorities (Herr, 1989; Leong, 1995; Leung, 1995; Robinson & Howard-Hamilton, 2000; Sue & Sue, 1999; Wehrly, Kenney, & Kenney, 1999), women (Arrendondo, 1992; Betz & Fitzgerald, 1997), older adults (Brewington & Nassar-Mcmillan, 2000; Waters & Goodman, 1990), persons with disabilities (Enright, Conyers, & Szymanski, 1996) and minority populations based on sexual orientation including gay, lesbian, and bisexual persons (Gelbert & Chojnacki, 1996). Other models for career interventions would include active engagement (Amundson, 1997), narrative-based career counseling (Cochran, 1997; Jepsen, 1995; Savickas, 1997), career development for women (Betz & Fitzgerald, 1997; Fassinger, 1998; Worell & Etaugh, 1994), spirituality and career development (Bloch & Richmond, 1997, 1998), transition counseling (Feller & Walz, 1996; Schlossberg, Waters, & Goodman, 1995), holistic life planning (Hansen, 1997), sociodynamic/ constructivist counseling (Peavy, 1994), positive uncertainty (Gellatt, 1989), and planned happenstance (Mitchell, Levin, & Krumboltz, 1999). Further, career intervention models for gay and lesbian clients (Pope, 1995) and career interventions tailored to personality style (Kjos, 1996) also appear in the literature. While space in this article does not permit an overall appraisal of all career interventions, the career literature contains many interventions intended to address the needs of diverse groups of people in the workforce.

One notable study addressed the question of which interventions would be effective in fostering the vocational development of disadvantaged or minority groups. Rodriguez and Blocker (1988) compared two career interventions designed to enhance the career maturity of Puerto

Rican women attending an urban college. They concluded that traditional career interventions, when they are carefully designed, can produce significant results with a population whose background and prior experiences may differ profoundly from that of typical middle-class clients.

In a review of the status of contemporary counseling, Herr (1989) described at-risk populations to be one of the four major challenges facing the counseling profession. The other three were (1) the psychological effects of advanced technology, (2) the changing American family, and (3) cultural diversity. Herr reviewed subgroups found to be at-risk for developing mental or educational disorders, and expanded the concept of at-risk status beyond prevailing school definitions. Career issues were embedded in Herr's discussion, but they were not the major focus. Research clearly supports the contention that students from impoverished or minority backgrounds will be more susceptible to career difficulties later in life (Gottfredson, 1986). Furthermore, demographers seem certain that African Americans, Hispanics, and Asians will be the fastest growing segment of the labor force for years to come (Fullerton, 1989). By the year 2008, Hispanic, nonHispanic African Americans, Asians, and other racial groups are projected to comprise an increasing share of the labor force, while the percent of white, nonHispanic persons in the labor force will decrease from 73.9 to 70.7% (Bureau of Labor Statistics, 2000). Research addressing career counseling for diverse populations is not yet as frequent or comprehensive as needed (McBride, 2001). Given the changing demographics of our society, it is clear that more attention must be paid to the career development of at-risk and minority populations.

Bloch (1989a) surveyed 1,584 career information system sites in 11 states to ascertain how they were serving at-risk youth. Thirteen model programs were identified that, on the basis of survey results, produced beneficial client outcomes such as promotion to the next grade, reduction in course failures, increased retention, increased options, knowledge and understanding of the world of work, and increased motivation, self-awareness, and self-esteem.

Brown, Minor, and Jepsen (1991) report from a national Gallup poll of a representative sample of 1,006 American adults reminds us that although career concerns are widespread, most Americans are doing well in coping with their difficulties. Nearly 60% of respondents reported little or no job stress during that past year, and a remarkable 86% reported that their skills and abilities were being used very well or fairly well on the job. And, as Drier (1989) noted, "Interventions have been reasonably successful in assisting individuals who do have problems."

However, the data from the Gallup poll are disturbing when one examines the responses of some at-risk populations (e.g., African Americans) to the poll. For instance, whereas only 50%–60% of respondents surveyed would get more career information if they could do it over, nearly 79% of African Americans who were surveyed would do so (Brown et al., 1991). In nearly every category, Arbona (1990) indicated that African Americans (Hispanic respondents were too few and were eliminated, but are clearly at risk) indicated greater levels of career concerns than did Caucasians. These data suggest serious problems in light of the relatively few practitioners who reported seeing African American or minority clients. Those populations most in need of career services may be those least likely to receive them.

The intervention method clearly affects the attractiveness, if not the outcome, of most therapeutic interventions for minority clients. For example, Szapocznik et al. (1989) found that structural family therapy was more effective in maintaining the integrity of Hispanic families than was a psychodynamic approach, reinforcing previous suggestions that highly structured approaches to therapeutic intervention may be more beneficial for minority clients. Although Casas and Arbano (1992) described career-related issues faced by Hispanics, it should be noted that little work has been done to design career development systems with the needs of at-risk populations in mind (Hawks & Muha, 1991). In regards to career interventions and assessment with culturally different clients, the call for more research cannot really be overexaggerated given the dearth of empirical data on the topic. If we accept the central role that cultural orientation plays in vocational behavior in general and career counseling in particular, then there is a need to continue to examine the cultural validity of the dominate Eurocentric theories for culturally different clients (Leong, 1995).

The career literature encourages separate treatment of special groups, and recognition of their unique needs and problems. This trend is appropriate in view of the limited attention to special groups in the career literature, and has been an important corrective step toward addressing the continuing lack of services available to these underserved populations (Spokane, 1989). Separate treatment increases sensitivity to the needs of others, but may obscure any underlying similarities in the experiences of at-risk group members (Subich, 1989). Separate treatment may also result in a fracturing of the core aspects of vocational behavior and may lead to more, not less, confusion about how to meet the needs of special groups (Spokane, 1989). Szymanski and Hanley-Maxwell (1996) proposed an ecological model of career development for persons with developmental disabilities. The ecological model incorporates the factors important in career interventions regardless of intellectual ability including: family, education, planning, functional curriculum, and choice. Interventions focus on individual factors (i.e., aptitudes), contextual factors (i.e., labor market), meaning factors (i.e., values), work environment factors (i.e., adaptations), and output factors (i.e., productivity expectations). Solly (1987) also proposed a workable intervention model for the mentally disabled.

Harding (1986) attributed the similarity in perspectives and values of at-risk groups to the shared effects of reactions to the dominant Caucasian culture. Indeed, evidence on differences in the occupational interests of special groups does suggest more. At risk groups were attracted more to social and enterprising interests and had fewer investigative interests. The observation could also apply to gender differences in interests as well, and which may also be the result of a general need to anticipate and to adapt to a powerful dominant culture (Spokane, 1989).

Social constraints seem to have common effects on many special groups. Specifically, such constraints seem to:

1.   Limit consideration of certain careers (less investigative, more social);

2.   Reduce the expectation and the likelihood that stated aspirations will be attained at the level stated;

3.   Increase the number of factors considered when making career choices, and increase the salience of external factors;

4.   Increase the need for highly structured interventions to overcome social constraints;

5.   Increase the stress levels on all family members, but especially on working women and minority group members (Spokane, 1989).

According to survey findings, the most common problems presented by the clients were: (a) making a career choice or finding a direction (19%), (b) conflicts in the workplace (13%), (c) family conflicts (9%), (d) self-occupational knowledge (8%), and (e) indecision 8% (Spokane, 1989).

Finding a vocational direction has been reported as the most basic of presenting problems. Osipow (1989) called this problem a lack of structure. Simply stated, the client has little or no idea (schema) about how to make a career choice, nor any content area in which to make one. Thus, the problem was seen to mean a lack of vocational identity (Holland, Daiger, & Power, 1980) or a suspension of that identity in the face of conflict or compromise, rather than an inability to make a conscious selection among available career options. The career literature contains some interesting attempts to understanding the cognitive and emotional processes involved in forging a vocation schema.

Blustein (1989) found that the exploratory behavior of those participants who had well formed identities was focused on the environment (options exploration) whereas those individuals still struggling with the planning process were focused on an internal search (self-exploration). Blustein concluded that internal exploration may be more useful in the early stages of vocational development and external exploration in the latter stages. In a related study, Blustein, Devenis, and Kidney (1989) gave college students a measure of Marcia's (1966) ego identity status, and measures of exploratory activity and decisional status (commitment). A canonical analysis confirmed that Marcia's moratorium condition was related to a lack of occupational commitment, and that career exploration was positively associated with Marcia's moratorium and identity-achieved positions and inversely related to identity diffusion. Blustein, Devenis, and Kidney (1989) suggested that clients be encouraged to explore both vocational and nonvocational life domains together. In a review of the identity status literature, illustrated with case histories, Raskin (1989) made a similar point namely that career development and identity development are parallel processes.

In a somewhat similar vein, a series of studies (Baehr & Orban, 1989; Barak, Librowsky, & Shilop, 1989; Lapan, Boggs, & Morrill, 1989; Lent, Larkin, & Brown, 1989; Lopez, 1989; Neimeyer, Brown, Metzler, Hagans, & Tangue, 1989; Smart, 1989) examined the development of vocational interests and personality. Barak et al. (1989) elaborated on an earlier model to test the view that interests are not simply learned dispositions, but are mediated by complex cognitive processes. Two simultaneous cognitive processes are used in developing career interests: (a) self-schemata, which are similar to self-efficacy and task approach skills, and (b) expectations about future successful performance. Barak et al. (1989) found strong correlations among three variables: expected success, perceived ability, and anticipated satisfaction, and in a second study, found a strong correlation between perceived abilities and actual abilities. Similarly, Lent et al. (1989) found that all three scale types on the SCII (Holland themes, basic interest scores, occupational scales) were moderately correlated with estimates of engineering and science self-efficacy. Lent et al. (1989) suggested that self-efficacy may be both an antecedent to and a consequence of science interests. In a study very similar to Lent et al. (1989) Lapan, Boggs, and Morrill (1989) found a science and technical interest factor that was mediated by mathematic self-efficacy and high school mathematics preparation.

Families affect career decisions as they are being made, but they also seem to directly affect the formulation of vocational interests. Smart (1989) tested a causal model of the development of Holland types using Astin's longitudinal CIRP data on 2,618 male and female college students. Smart found several variables that exerted a direct but complex influence on eventual Holland types, including family background, personal career aspirations, and the kind of college attended. Lopez (1989) proposed a family dynamics model of vocational identity and found that degree of psychological separation; martial conflict, trait anxiety, and academic adjustment were all significant predictors of vocational identity. Finally, Chusid and Cochran (1989) used interviews to show that family dynamics may be reenacted in workplace conflicts.

Gottfredson's (1981) heuristic model of circumscription and compromise was operationlized in two direct, independent, empirical tests. Noting the methodological difficulties involved in studying the compromise process (which is often examined after it has already occurred), Holt (1989) compared forced and free choice methods for ascertaining whether engineering and social work students ranked jobs using status and interest area. Although it was assumed that all incumbents in social work were S type and those in engineering were I types, which is rarely true (Aranya, Barak, & Amernic, 1981), it was clear, as least for engineers, that interests did not always dictate preference.

The centric model of career counseling was developed for use in employment counseling (Amundson, 1987, 1989). This approach takes into account psychological, social, and economic factors, and work is viewed as one part of a total lifestyle. The centric career counseling model uses four developmental phases to describe the counseling process. Progress involves back and forth movement through the phases and the use of various structured activities within a humanistic counseling context. Expansion is needed at the exploration and assessment phase, contraction occurs as people evaluate and commit to options, further expansion and flexibility become necessary as these options are imbedded within a fast-changing labor market.

Lack of knowledge was addressed in several contributions, and overlaps with the area of career information. A useful contribution to this area is the distinction that Moses (1989) makes between career and occupational information, but perhaps more important is the need to differentiate information about occupations or careers from information about how one would feel when doing an occupation—which is the essence of most career decisions. Kuhn (1989) reviewed evidence for the notion that individuals act as intuitive or personal scientists concerning their own lives, and noted that when evidence does not fit a theory, the individual will either revise the theory or collect different evidence to bolster the theory. The social psychology of personal career information acquisition and absorption was addressed by several authors (Gati & Tikotski, 1989; Helwig, Hiatt, & Vidales, 1989; Neimeyer et. al., 1989).

In a special issue of the *Journal of Career Development*, Pallas, Natriello, and McDill (1989) reviewed studies using personal construct theory to assess the personal meaning of work. Wolleat (1989) argued that gender plays a significant role in most information schemata and should be a fundamental part of, rather than a moderator of, career information processing. Olson, McWhirter, and Horan (1989) elaborated a four-stage model of decision making during career counseling (conceptualization, enlargement of response repertoire, identification of discriminative stimuli, and response selection). Bloch (1989b) asked two fundamental questions about the nature of information search and retrieval: How do people acquire and use information? How does career information become career knowledge?

Increasingly, we are convinced that individuals are systematic and scientific in formulating hypotheses about the world of work and testing them against naive personal theories about the way careers are or should be (Spokane, 1989).

Indecision—its nature, correlates and causes, continue to receive steady attention in the literature. Newman, Fuqua, and Seaworth (1989) offered six possible models of the relationship between anxiety and career indecision. Three of these models posit direct linear relationships between anxiety and indecision, whereas three posit more complex reciprocal relationships. The six models that were clearly portrayed in the figure are:

1. Indecision produces indecision;
2. Anxiety produces indecision;
3. Inadequate identity information produces anxiety which then results in career indecision;
4. Inadequate identity concurrently produces both indecision and anxiety;
5. Anxiety and indecision are reciprocally related;
6. Anxiety, identity, and indecision are reciprocal.

Indecision, according to Newman et al. (1989) is not a simple problem, and may not follow the same model in every individual.

Gellatt (1989) acknowledged substantial advances in human decision processing that force reconsideration of simple rational career decision models. Flexible decision models that include emotional valence, and incorporate disconfirming information as a crucial aspect of the decision process, are more consistent with social psychological modes of career decision-making (Gellat, 1989; Heppner, 1989).

Although vocational identity (knowing one's aptitudes, skills, and interest), took the top three ranks in the literature, personal appearance, selling one's skills, a properly completed application relating personal qualities to the job demands, ability to do well in a job interview, and knowing what personal characteristics were very important to employers and were therefore also critical skills for finding a job (Spokane & Hawks, 1990).

A consistent theme emerges from the review of common client presenting problems. Most clients will agonize over identity issues, including some that are longstanding, as a preview to sifting through the internal and external information about various career options. Using an iterative process, they will then add, delete, or revise those options until a reasonable compromise between individual aspirations and social constraints is achieved and a commitment is made to pursue a limited set of options in depth (Spokane, 1989).

Newer trait-factor models (Betz, Fitzgerald, & Hill, 1989) and some development theories view career decisions as usually discrete, even if gradual. But career decisions seem to acquire a transactional, fluid quality during career intervention. These transactions are moderated by personality style and in particular by self-esteem (Bednar, Wells, & Peterson, 1989; Kernis, Brockner, & Frankel, 1989) and anxiety. The anguishing quality of these decisions reinforces the need for application of advanced counseling skills (e.g., probing, clarification) to understand not only what clients say during career interventions, but what are often deeply felt beliefs, covered by a socially acceptable veneer, or, even left unsaid (Krumboltz, 1983).

In another vein, the literature revealed that individual counseling was by far the most common intervention mode (74%), followed by computer interventions (12.5%), consultation (10.2%), and workshops or seminars (10.0%) (Spokane, 1989). More recently, Sampson, Readon, Peterson, & Lenz (2003) concluded the following relative to the effects of career interventions:

1. group counseling or class interventions are more effective than individual counseling;
2. Oliver and Spokane (1988)—career classes have the greatest impact on client gains, but are most expensive;
3. individualized and structured group interventions are most cost-effective.

Two contributions discussed models and issues in individual career counseling. The first by Amundson (1989) described the process by which an individual first expands, using exploration and assessment, and then narrows the range of alternatives under consideration during career counseling. The client then makes a commitment that may involve compromise and integration of needs and expectation with labor market constraints, finally launching an implementation or action plan.

Second, Savickas (1989b) described an Adlerian enhancement of the traditional matching model of career counseling, which stresses belongingness rather than fit, uniqueness rather then similarity, career paths rather than interests, and private logic rather than discrete choices. Savickas elaborated what he called career style assessment and counseling based on Adlerian psychology, which helps the client to examine the unfolding of a career lifestyle as the basis for intervention.

Case studies are a relatively recent phenomenon that is having a powerful effect on the practice of counseling in general and perhaps on career counseling as well. Hill (1989) draws on a decade empirical work on therapist intentions and client reactions to analyze eight case studies of psychotherapy. Yalom (1989) employed existential theory to provide a rich and interesting description of cases on a more personal level. Two specific career case studies were found in the literature. The first was a study of a PhD candidate in chemistry reconsidering his choice (Freemont, 1989; Litak, 1989; Moses, 1989), and the second a case of an adult returning to a university to train as a teacher (Greeley, 1989; Nile, 1989; Toman, 1989).

The second most common intervention strategy, computer interventions, appeared in several studies and articles (Bloch & Kinnison, 1989; Bradshaw, 1996; Garis & Hess, 1989; Gati & Tikotski, 1989; Kapes, Borman, & Frazier, 1989; Stewart, 1989). A guide by Walz and Bleuer (1989) reviewed software on career selection and job readiness, resume writing, and job search (Sampson, 1989), and contains a brief but thorough discussion of trends in software for career counseling by Bridges (1989). Finally, Sampson (1989) offered a model of information processing during computer-assisted career guidance that includes knowledge, decision making, and executive processing or metacognitions, and interventions to facilitate information processing.

In one of the few empirical studies on computer-based intervention, Kapes, Borman, and Frazier (1989) randomly assigned students in multiple sections of a semester-long career class to either System of Interactive and Guidance and Information (SIGI) or Discover for an average of 4.4 hours. Multiple measures of decisional status and user satisfaction were used in a regression analysis to evaluate the effects of the computer experience. Although no control group was utilized (a common weakness in computer intervention studies), respondents, in this otherwise well developed study showed across-the-board improvements in decisional status (Spokane, 1989). Technological advances in career intervention, especially computer-assisted guidance and the ubiquitous involvement of the internet in career information dissemination call for enhanced sophistication in the delivery of career services (Hansen, 2000).

DeLucia, Black, Longhead, and Hultsman (1989) described a stepped approach (increasing intensity) to career intervention that began with minimal educational intervention and progressed through media-based intervention, brief contact, group counseling, and finally to therapeutically-based individual counseling. These model-building efforts are of some benefit, but the career literature was surprisingly devoid of empirical studies of individual or group counseling and could represent a downward trend in the frequency of empirical evaluation studies (Spokane, 1989).

Buescher, Johnston, Lucas, and Hughey (1989) evaluated a 1 1/2 hour early informational intervention for college students that included a card sort and found significant increases in vocational identity for participants compared to nontreated controls. Catron and Catron (1989) described a program for parents to help them understand the feelings they have when their son or daughter is a freshman, and to try to establish an adult relationship with their freshmen children.

Relative to the career counselor's professional role in the process, Tennyson, Miller, Skovholt, and Williams (1989) asked 163 counselors in Minnesota how often they performed career guidance, including evaluation and assessment. Counselors in senior high schools spent more time in career guidance roles, whereas those in junior highs were involved in developmental guidance, but only in a limited way. Montana (1989) found that business schools were heavily invested (64%) in career planning and developmental instruction.

Fundamental skills analysis and mental imagery and feedback from testing (functional analysis of skills, strengths, interests, and values) were favored techniques used by counselors. A review of the use of mental imagery in career intervention by Skovholt, Morgan, and Negron-Cunningham (1989) concluded that daydreams were not only valid predictors of occupational choice, but also that the limited evidence confirms the effectiveness of imagery as a career intervention technique. Two forms of imagery were described: guided imagery and induced relaxation with scripting. Other favorite intervention techniques were (1) mental imagery, fantasy, or cognitive rehearsal of aspirations, (2) feedback from testing, (3) job shadowing, interviewing, (4) card sorts, (5) options generation and evaluation, (5) Adlerian/family techniques, (6) referral, (7) rational problem solving, (8) goal setting, (9) self-assessment, and (10) general feedback (Spokane, 1989).

The literature suggests that we do not embrace clear models of the career intervention process, and that we should probably devote more attention to the development and validation of such models (Spokane, 1989). Hershenson, Power, and Seligman (1989) provided a compelling set of three models (diagnostic and treatment planning, minority group status, personal and environmental coping) for mental health counseling that, in some ways, are suggestive of the models that career intervention might emulate. In the diagnostic and treatment planning model, the counselor collects and evaluates data and plans an intervention for the client. In the second, minority group status model, the clients' culture and environment are the central focus of intervention, and the third model (P-E coping) is a developmental view that strives to understand and improve how people interact with various environments.

Some are concerned that career intervention still over utilizes the diagnostic and treatment models. The assumptions suggest a model in which the first step is to develop an expectation on the client's and the counselor's parts that a reasonably solution can be found, followed by specific attempts to encourage or mobilize the client to engage in constructive behavior that will result in a positive career outcome. Sampson et al. (2003) suggests that there are few useful accountability and evaluative models. Accountability models are hampered by the absence of conceptual and operational constructs that define outputs of career service interventions, for example, How do career services change the lives of clients?

Though career counseling is a vigorous, growing, and sophisticated field, current practices reflect a reliance on the familiar and the comfortable, and researchers in the field have failed to conduct empirical investigation of career intervention models and processes. What counselors do in practice seems more provincial than what is written in the literature. Current practice does not reflect all of the advances in the field of vocational behavior, nor does it seem particularly responsive to pressing societal needs covered in the literature (e.g., other at-risk groups, prevention, and consultation). Nonetheless, the profession seems to be nearing some definitive answers regarding the nature of career problems and the most effective ways to remediate them.

Although some career problems are simple ones, most adult career problems and decisions are increasingly seen as complex social psychological events that require professional skill to resolve. They may or may not also be mental health problems. Fortunately, we have a large and sophisticated array of intervention techniques and devices with which to address these problems. The next generation of career intervention research will probably be an exciting blend of group and single case data that builds on the substantial research based of nearly 100 years of research, theory, and practice.

Individual career counseling practice, still conducted largely in dyadic interviews, is benefiting from the case study emphasis in counseling and therapy generally. We will see more of this rich and complex methodology applied to career cases in the future, and the result will likely be clearer, more practical models of the career intervention process. Computers are becoming a standard intervention component, and clients now expect and want such an intervention. The next generation of computer hardware and software should accelerate the adoption of these methods. Although individual counseling is still the prime mode of intervention, the literature reflects a need for a more diverse array of intervention strategies and efforts, especially to address the needs of at-risk groups (Spokane, 1989).

Self-efficacy expectations, when viewed in relation to careers, refer to a person's beliefs regarding "career-related behaviors, educational and occupational choice, and self-efficacy expectations, and when viewed in relation to careers, refer to a person's beliefs regarding, and performance and persistence in the implementation of those choices" (Betz & Hackett, 1997, p. 383). They are reflected in an individual's perception about his or her ability to perform a given task or behavior (efficacy expectation) and his or her belief about the consequences of behavior or performance (outcome expectation) (Hackett & Betz, 1981).

CONTEMPORARY CAREER INTERVENTION MODELS: HOW FAR HAVE THEY EVOLVED?

The social cognitive career theory (SCCT) developed by Lent, Hackett, and Brown (1996) draws on Bandura's self-efficacy theory. It offers a framework for career development, explaining the interplay between educational and vocational interests, career-related choices, and performance. SCCT highlights the relationship among social cognitive variables (e.g., self-efficacy) and their relationship with other variables in the individual's sociocontextual environment, such as gender, race/culture, family, community, and political components. Chen (1997) contends that this integration of self and social context offers an opportunity for individuals to gain a sense of control over their career development and increase their career-related self-efficacy expectations.

During the early development of career counseling models, the trait-and-factor approach received the most attention and has survived as a viable part of current trait-oriented models. In fact, Brown and Brooks (1991) point out that it still may be the most popular theory among contemporary models. During the last decade there has been a gradual convergence of trait-and-factor methods and procedures with person-environment-fit constructs also referred to as person-environment-correspondence in its early development (Rounds & Tracey, 1990). The current model includes (1) both cognitive and affective processes; (2) clinical information and qualitative data in the appraisal process; and (3) the counselor's role has shifted from a directive approach to one in which counselor and client negotiate and collaborate (Swanson, 1996).

The Developmental Model originated from the premise that career development is a lifelong process and the career counseling needs of individuals must be met at all stages in life (Healy, 1982). The development of goals, learning strategies, and the timing of interventions in this model are guided by Super's (1957, 1990) vocational developmental tasks and stages. The overall goals are problem identification and developing intervention strategies to overcome them. The Developmental Model also stresses the necessity of discovering each client's uniqueness of development (Zunker, 2002).

A learning theory of career counseling emphasizes that each individual's unique learning experiences over the life span are most influential in the career choice process (Krumboltz, 1996; Krumboltz & Hamel, 1977; Krumboltz, Mitchell, & Gelatt, 1975; Krumboltz & Nichols, 1990; and Mitchell & Krumboltz, 1990, 1996). In this model, the client is viewed as one who is exploring and experimenting with possibilities and tentative decisions (Zunker, 2002). In fact, Krumboltz (1996) strongly suggests that clients do not need to make a career decision for the sake of deciding, but rather should be encouraged to explore, eliminate, and make tentative tryouts in a learning process that leads toward progress accomplishing their personal goals.

The Cognitive Information Processing Model (CIP) requires an in-depth understanding of cognitive information process theory, and information processing for the CIP also requires an in-depth understanding of CIP theory. Information processing for career decision making is conceptualized within this model as a hierarchical system from a base of knowledge domains (self knowledge and occupational knowledge) to a decision skills domain and finally to an executive processing domain (Zunker, 2002). Within the framework of the CIP approach, readiness is defined as the capability of an individual to make appropriate career choices, taking into account the complexity of family, social, economic, and organizational factors that influence an individual's career development. Another way to viewing these two dimensions is that capability represents internal factors and complexity represents external factors that influence an individual's ability to make appropriate career choices (Sampson, Peterson, Reardon, & Lenz, 2000).

Career counseling group interventions using cognitive instruction have been recommended for youth. Such group interventions are especially recommended for youth with learning disabilities (e.g., Biller, 1987). In cognitive instruction, counselors and teachers provide clear explanations and models of behaviors and thinking that students may not be able to develop spontaneously. Students practice with peers in pairs and small groups, adapting the problem-solving approaches and explanations of the teacher to develop their own understanding (Englert, Tarrant, & Mariage, 1992).

In cognitively-based instruction, problem solving and other complex thinking skills have a central place. Rather than absorbing facts, students make sense of what they are taught and construct their own knowledge (Hutchinson & Freeman, 1994). Students learn when they are cognitively engaged as they work with ideas and actively use information as it is acquired. In the classroom, cognitive approaches involve students interacting with each other. Thinking about their answers and giving explanations for their thinking helps students realize there are a number of ways of arriving at understanding. Moreover, negotiating meaning, listening to colleagues, and arriving at consensus are skills required in the modern workplace.

The WonderTech Work Skills Simulation (Cairns & Woodard, 1994) is a classroom simulation, which is useful in assisting adolescents and young adults to learn work transition skills. It incorporates the requirements outlined above through the provision of a complex, interactive structure that provides students with experience in completing job applications, participating effectively in job interviews, and practicing job performance. The simulation focuses on the development of five skill sets which are considered essential by employers, counselors, and employees including: basic academic skills (literacy/numeracy), self-management skills, problem-solving skills, co-operative action or teamwork skills, and leadership or initiative-taking skills.

Self-directed career decision making can be used as a cost-effective delivery methods for career service interventions (Reardon, 1996). Experience has also shown that career service interventions in the self-directed career decision-making mode tend to be more successful when participants make specific recommendations about resource use than to identify user needs (Sampson et al., 2002).

A growing awareness among practitioners of emerging demographics that will produce a more racial and ethnically diverse workforce strongly reinforces the need for modifying career counseling models. Research that addresses the career counseling needs of multicultural groups is in its infancy, although there have been significant increases in numbers (Biller, 1987). Increasing attention is being given to preparing counselors to work with culturally different clients relative to vocational interests in a traditional-minded population (Isaacson & Brown, 1997). Arbona (1996) lists numerous publications that focus on multicultural issues in career counseling.

A review of the literature reveals numerous and varied career counseling interventions. Benzanson and Reilly (1998) focus on the best and most effective interventions that are available to help clients learn to manage their work life and work futures successfully. Using vocational assessment feedback to help use self-knowledge as an intervention in career decision-making was proposed by Kneishok, Ulneir, Hecox, and Welterstein (2000). Interventions using announcements, handouts and computer-assisted career guidance were addressed by Peterson, Long, & Bippuos (1999). Dykerman and Herr (2001) identified four clusters of career development interventions: work based interventions, advising interventions, introductory interventions, and curriculum based interventions. Other authors measured the effects of interventions on career progress (Barnes & Herr, 1998). Gender differences were addressed by Valentine (1998). Career development interventions used in United States secondary schools were presented by Wonacott (2001). Career intervention models including technical skills training interventions were described by Petridor and Spathes (2001) and Bernes and Magnusson (1999) discusses organizational career interventions.

EXPANDED COUNSELOR ROLES

In a recent publication, Harmon (1996) suggests that the gap between counseling skills and the current needs of a changing diverse society has increased, making it imperative for counselors to upgrade their training. Clearly, future career counselors should not only be familiar with career development research but also with effective techniques, procedures, and materials used in contemporary models that can be used for building new approaches for the future. As the science of career development expands and the forms of career intervention become more comprehensive, the role of career counselors will increasingly involve planning of customized programs tailored to the populations and settings in which the career counselors serve, and will include applying behavioral science to the match of career interventions to career concerns, and systematically use technologies to complement individual or group approaches to the practice of career development (Herr, 2000). The counselor's role will include: (1) developing and clarifying self concepts, (2) relating occupational information to self-information, (3) teaching decision-making skills, (4) providing opportunities for occupational reality testing, and (5) assisting individuals in educational and occupational placement (Sampson et. al., 2003).

CONCLUSION

A growing scientific base demonstrates that a wide range of career guidance and career counseling interventions have positive effects across subpopulations and settings on career information deficits, career awareness and exploration, client needs for support, career planning skills and personal and interpersonal work skills (Campbell, Connell, Boyle, & Bhaerman, 1983; Oliver & Spokane, 1988; Sexton, Whiston, Bleuer, & Walz, 1997; Spokane & Oliver, 1983). Other significant research summaries have shown that effective career intervention consists of specific elements including: (1) occupational information organized by a comprehensive method and easily accessible to a client, (2) assessment materials and devices that clarify a client's self-picture and vocational potentials, (3) individual or group activities that provide a rehearsal of career plans or problems, (4) counselors, groups, or peers that provide support, and (5) a comprehensive cognitive structure for organizing information about self and occupational alternatives (Holland, Mongoon, & Spokane, 1981). It has become increasingly apparent that for persons who have experienced major work adjustment problems, unusual job stress, involuntary unemployment and underemployment, career counseling cannot be separated from personal counseling (Herr, 1998) and interventions must address personal issues.

Dykerman and Herr (2001) also stated that the lack of a comprehensive organization of interventions makes quality research and program evaluation difficult. Each year millions of state and federal education funds are spent on career development interventions. However, no uniform nomenclature, definition, and organization of these interventions exist in the professional literature. The lack of specificity about interventions in the career development and academic literature is a problem. Counselors need concrete guidance on what career interventions can give the most leverage in promoting effective career services (National Research Center for Career and Technical Education, 2001). The research literature also indicates a lack of methodologically sound career intervention studies (Prideaux, Creed, Muller, & Patton, 2001).

RECOMMENDATIONS

Future career counseling research must include more rigorous evaluations of all types of career interventions and of how each type of intervention actually works. Examination of linkages between client goals and differential career process effectiveness is needed to define a client treatment interaction matrix that effectively summarizes what is known about outcomes of particular interventions, conditions under which these outcomes are achieved, and client populations for whom such interventions are most effective (McBride, 2001). In the future, it will be useful to take an aggregate view of the theoretical constructs available, the populations to which they apply and their implications for different systems of interventions. These insights need to be placed into a matrix that summarizes what we know about career behavior, the relationship of theoretical constructs to categories of presenting problems by client type, setting, intervention, and by likely behavioral outcomes. Such a matrix would essentially synthesize and map the scientific base related to both career theory and practice and make such a knowledge base accessible to counselors (Herr & Cramer, 1996). As stated by (Brown & Krane, 2000), effective interventions have five common elements.

1. allow the client to clarify career and life goals in writing;
2. provide clients with individualized interpretations and feedback, for example, test results;
3. provide current information on risks and rewards of selected occupations;
4. include a study of models and mentors; and
5. assist in developing support networks for pursuing career aspirations.

Career counseling is one of many interventions that can be used to enhance the development of and/or change of career behavior. Therefore, research on career counseling is important, but complex. Research studies have demonstrated that career questions and concerns of the child, the adolescent, the young, midcareer, and older adults are, in general, developmentally different and require career guidance and counseling interventions that differ in language and content (Herr, 2000). Research is needed that distinguishes the effectiveness and outcomes of different approaches to career counseling as well as comparisons of career counseling to other career interventions. Future directions should include greater attention to cost-benefit ratios, comparative outcomes, and use of innovative research methodologies (Herr & Cramer, 1996). While traditional congruence models and interventions of matching individuals and jobs probably will be part of career development and planning, the complexity of career decision-making in the new millennium calls for the broadest possible definition of the term (McDaniel, 2000), and, more importantly, translating the broader concept into practice, interventions, and counselor preparation is imperative (Hansen, 2000). Combining quantitative and qualitative research approaches will provide rich descriptions of settings, cultures, and individual characteristics which mediate theoretical predictions and the viability of interventions. Such concerns will need to look at such questions as cost-benefit ratios for different career interventions (e.g., individual or group counseling, planned programs of career guidance or career education, computer-assisted career guidance systems, and the Internet) as well as under what conditions and for whom career counseling and personal counseling should be treated as separate interventions or fused (Herr & Cramer, 1996).

REFERENCES

Amundson, N. E. (1987). A visual means of organizing career information. *Journal of Employment Counseling, 24,* 2-7.

Amundson, N. E. (1998). A model of individual career counseling. *Journal of Employment Counseling, 26,* 132-138.

Amundson, N. E. (1995). *A centric career counseling model.* Greensboro, NC. (ERIC Document Reproduction Service No. ED 404 582).

Amundson, N. E. (1997). *Active engagement—Enhancing the career counseling process.* Richmond, BC: Ergon Communications.

Aranya, N., Barak, A., & Amernic, J. (1981). A test of Holland's theory in a population of accountants. *Journal of Vocational Behavior, 19,* 15-24.

Arbona, C. (1990). Career counseling research and Hispanics: A review of the literature. *The Counseling Psychologist, 18*(2), 300-323.

Arbona, C. (1996). Career theory and practice in a multicultural content. In M. L. Savickas & W. B. Walsh (Eds), *Handbook of career counseling theory and practice* (pp. 45-55). Palo Alto, CA: Davies-Black.

Arrendondo, P. (1992). Promoting the empowerment of women through counseling interventions. *Counseling and Human Development, 24*(8), 1-12.

Baehr, M. E., & Orban, J. A. (1989). The role of intellectual abilities and personality characteristics in determining success in higher level positions. *Journal of Vocational Behavior, 35,* 270- 287.

Baker, S. B., & Popowicz, C. L. (1983). Meta-analysis as a strategy for evaluating effects of career education interventions. *Vocational Guidance Quarterly, 31,* 178-186.

Barak, A., Librowsky, I., & Shilop, S. (1989). Cognitive determinates of interests: An extension of a theoretical model and initial empirical examination. *Journal of Vocational Behavior, 34,* 318-334.

Barnes, J., & Herr E. (1998). The effects of interventions on career development. *Journal of Career Development, 24,* 3, 179-93.

Bednar, R. L., Wells, M. G., & Peterson, S. R. (1989). *Self-esteem: Paradoxes and innovation in clinical theory and practice*: Washington, DC: American.

Bernes, K., & Magnusson, K. (1999, March). *Career paths and organizational development: Expanding alliances.* Paper presented at the annual conference of the National Consultation on Career Development, Ottawa, Canada.

Betz, N. E., & Fitzgerald, L. (1997). *The career psychology of women.* Orlando, FL: Academic Press.

Betz, N. E., Fitzgerald, L. F., & Hill, R. E. (1989). Trait-factor theories: Traditional cornerstone of career theory. In M. Arthur, D. T. Hall, & B. S. Lawrence (Eds.), *Handbook of career theory* (pp. 26-40). Cambridge, England: Cambridge University Press.

Betz, N. E., & Hackett, G. (1997, Fall). Applications of self-efficacy theory to the career assessment of women. *Journal of Career Assessment, 5*(4), 383-402.

Bezanson, L., & Reilly E. (1998). Choosing employment interventions: A guide for the discriminating palate. *Canadian Career Development Foundation*. Ottawa, Ontario, Canada.

Biller, E. F. (1987). *Career decision making for adolescents and young adults with learning disabilities: Theory, research, and practice*. Springfield, IL: Charles C. Thomas.

Bloch, D. P. (1989a). Using career information with dropouts and at-risk youth. *Career Development Quarterly, 21*, 177-187.

Bloch, D. P. (1989b). From career information to career knowledge: Self, search, and synthesis. *Journal of Career Development, 16*, 119-128.

Bloch, D. P., & Kinnison, J. F. (1989). A method for rating computer-based career information delivery systems. *Measurement and Evaluation in Counseling and Development, 21*, 177-187.

Bloch, D. P., & Richmond, L. J. (Eds.). (1997). *Connections between spirit and work in career development*. Palo Alto, CA: Davies-Black.

Bloch, D. P., & Richmond, L. J. (1998). *Soulwork—Finding the work you love, loving the work you have*. Palo Alto, CA: Davies-Black.

Blustein, D. L. (1989). The role of career exploration in the career-decision making of college students. *Journal of College Student Development, 30*, 111-117.

Blustein, D. L., Devenis, L. E., & Kidney, B. A. (1989). The development and validation of a two-dimensional model of the commitment to career choice process. *Journal of Vocational Behavior, 35*, 342-378.

Bradshaw, R. (1996). *Computer applications in career counseling*. Tallahassee: Florida State University. (ERIC Document Reproduction Service No. ED414415)

Brewington, J. O., & Nassar-McMillan, D. (2000, September). Older adults: Work related issues and implications for counseling. *Career Development Quarterly, 49*(1), 2-15.

Bridges, M. P. (1989). Software for career counseling. In G. R. Walz & J. C. Bleuer (Eds.), *Counseling software guide* (pp. 15-18). Alexandria, VA: American Association for Counseling and Development.

Brown, D., & Brooks, L. (1991). *Career counseling techniques*. Boston: Allyn & Bacon.

Brown, D., Minor, C. D. W., & Jepseps, D. (1991). The opinions of minorities about preparing for work: Report on the Second NCDA National Survey. *Career Development Quarterly, 41*(1), 5-19.

Brown, S. D., & Krane, R. (2000). Four (or five) sessions and a cloud of dust: Old assumptions and new observations about career counseling. In S. D. Brown & R. W. Lent (Eds.), *Handbook of counseling psychology* (3rd ed., pp. 740-766). New York: Wiley.

Buescher, K. L., Johnston, J. A., Lucas, E. B., & Hughey, K. F. (1989). Early intervention with undecided college students. *Journal of College Student Development, 30*, 375-376.

Bureau of Labor Statistics. (2000). *Report: Employment situation*. Washington, DC: Author.

Cairns, K. V., & Woodard, J. D. (1994). *WonderTech Work Skills Simulation*. Toronto, Ontario, Canada: Trifolium Books.

Campbell, R. E., Connell, J. B., Boyle, K. K., & Bhaerman, R. (1983). *Enhancing career development. Recommendations for action*. Columbus, OH: The National Center for Research in Vocational Education.

Casas, J. M., & Arbano, C. (1992). Hispanic career related issues and research: A diversity perspective. In D. Brown & C. W. Minor (Eds.), *Report of second Gallup survey: Focus on minorities* (pp. 36-52). Alexandria, VA: NCDA.

Catron, D. W., & Catron, S. S. (1989). Helping parents let go: A program for the parents of college freshmen. *Journal of College Student and Placement, 50*, 35-38.

Chen, C. P. (1997). Career projection: Narrative in context. *Journal of Vocational Education and Training. 49*(2), 311-326.

Chusid, H., & Cochran, L. (1989). Meaning of change from the perspective of family roles and dramas. *Journal of Counseling Psychology, 36*, 34-41.

Cochran, L. (1997). *Career counseling: A narrative approach*. Thousand Oaks, CA: Sage.

Delucia, J. L., Black, D. R., Loughead, T. A., & Hultsman, J. T. (1989). Purdue stepped approach model: Groups as symbiosis of career development and mental health counseling. *Journal of Career Development, 16*, 25-41.

Drier, H. N. (1989). Career development in education. In D. Brown & C. W. Minor (Eds.), *Working in America: A status report on planning and problems* (pp. 43-55). Alexandria, VA: National Career Development Association.

Dykeman, C., Ingram, M., Wood, C., Charles, S., Chen, M., & Herr, E. (2001). *The taxonomy of career development interventions that occur in America's secondary schools*. Greensboro, NC: ERIC Clearinghouse on Counseling and Student Services. (ERIC Document Reproduction Service No. ED475259)

Englert, C., Tarrant, K. L., & Mariage, T. V. (1992). Defining and redefining instructional practice in special education: Perspectives on good teaching. *Teacher Education and Special Education, 15*(2), 62-86.

Enright, M. S., & Conyers, L. M., & Szymanski, E. M. (1996, November, December). Career and career-related educational concerns of college students with disabilities. *Journal of Counseling and Development, 75*, 103-114.

Fassinger, R. E. (1998, August). *Gender as a factor in career services delivery: A modest proposal*. Paper presented at the annual convention of the American Psychological Association, San Francisco.

Feller, R., & Walz, G. (1996). *Career transitions in turbulent times: Exploring work, learning and careers*. Greenboro, NC: ERIC Clearinghouse on Counseling and Student Services. (ERIC Document Reproduction No. ED398519)

Freemont, S. K. (1989). Brillance and burnout: The case of Justin. *Career Development Quarterly, 37*, 298-301.

Fullerton, H. N. (1989, November). New labor force projections, spanning 1988–2000. *Monthly Labor Review*, 3-12.

Garis, I., & Hess, R. H. (1989). Career navigation: It's with college students beginning the job search process. *Career Development Quarterly, 38*, 65-74.

Gati, I., & Tikotsky, Y. (1989). Strategies for collection and processing of occupational information in making career decisions. *Journal of Counseling Psychology 36*, 430-439.

Gelbert, S., & Chojnacki, J. T. (1996). *Career and life planning with gay, lesbian, & bisexual persons*. Alexandria, VA: American Counseling Association.

Gellatt, H. B. (1989). Positive uncertainty: A new decision-making framework for counseling. *Journal of Counseling Psychology, 36,* 252-256.

Gottfredson, L. S. (1981). Circumscription and compromise: A developmental theory of occupational aspirations. *Journal of Counseling Psychology, 28,* 549-579.

Gottfredson, L. L. (1986). Special groups and the beneficial use of vocational interest inventories. In W. B. Walsh & S. H. Ospow (Eds.), *Advances in vocational psychology: The assessment of interests* (Vol. 1, pp. 127-198). Hillsdale, NJ: Erlbaum.

Greeley, A. T. (1989). A returning adult's struggle with wanting it all: The case of Fabian. *Career Development Quarterly, 38,* 33-38.

Hackett, G., & Betz, N. (1981, June). A self-efficacy approach to the career development of women. *Journal of Vocational Behavior 18*(3), 326-39.

Hansen, L. S. (1997). *Integrative life planning—Critical tasks for career development and changing life patterns*. San Francisco: Jossey-Bass.

Hansen, S. (2000, June). *Preparing counselors for career development in the new millennium*. Paper presented at National Career Development Conference, Pittsburgh, PA.

Harding, S. (1986). *The science question if feminism*. Ithaca. NY: Cornell University Press.

Harmon, L. W. (1996). A moving target: The widening gap between theory and practice. In M. L. Savickas & W. B. Welsh (Eds.), *Handbook for career counseling theory and practice* (pp. 37-45). Palo Alto. CA: Davies-Black.

Hawks, B. B., & Muha, D. (1991). Facilitating the career development of minorities: Doing it differently the second time. *Career Development Quarterly, 39,* 251-260.

Healy, C. C. (1982). *Career development: Counseling through life stages*. Boston: Allyn & Bacon.

Helwig, A. A., Hiatt, R., & Vidales, J. L. (1989). Job hunting: Critical knowledge and skills. *Journal of Career Development, 15,* 143-153.

Heppner, P. P. (1989). Identifying the complexities within clients' thinking and decision making. *Journal of Counseling Psychology, 36,* 257-259.

Hershenson, D. B., Power, P. W., & Seligman, L. (1989). Mental health counseling theory: Present status and future prospects. *Journal of Mental Health Counseling, 11,* 44-69.

Herr, E. L. (1989). *Counseling in a dynamic society: Opportunities and challenges*. Alexandria, VA: American Association for Counseling and Development.

Herr, E. L. (2000, June). *Perspectives on career development: The legacy of the 20th century—The innovation of the 21st*. Paper presented at NCDA past presidents Eminent Career Awardees Ceremony, Pittsburgh, PA.

Herr, E. L., & Cramer, S. H. (1996). *Career guidance and counseling through the lifespan. Systematic approaches* (5th ed.). New York: Harper Collins.

Hill, C. E. (1989). *Therapist techniques and client outcomes: Eight cases of brief psychotherapy*. Newbury Park, CA: Sage.

Holland, J. L., Daiger, D., & Power, P. (1980). *My vocational situation*. Palo Alto, CA: Consulting Psychologists Press.

Holland, J. L., Magoon, T. M., & Spokane, A. R. (1981). Counseling psychology: Career interventions, research, and theory. *Annual Review of Psychology, 32*, 279-300.

Holt, P. (1989). Differential effect of status and interest in the process of compromise. *Journal of Counseling Psychology, 36*, 42-47.

Hoyt, K. B. (1980). *Evaluation of K-12 career education: A status report*. Washington, DC: Office of Career Education.

Hutchinson, N. L., & Freeman, J. C. (1994). *Pathways (5 volumes)*. Toronto, Ontario, Canada: Nelson.

Isaacson, L., & Brown, D. (1997). *Career information, career counseling, and career development*. Boston: Allyn & Bacon.

Jepsen, D. (1995, June). *Career as a story: A narrative approach to career counseling*. Paper presented at the National Career Development Association Conference, San Francisco.

Kapes, J. T., Borman, C. A., & Frazier, N. (1989). An evaluation of the SIGI and Discover microcomputer-based career guidance systems. *Measurement and Evaluation in Counseling and Development, 22*, 126-136.

Kernis, M. H., Brockner, J., & Frankel, B. (1989). Self-esteem and reactions to failure: The mediating role of overgeneralization. *Journal of Personality and Social Psychology, 57*, 707-714.

Kjos, D. (1996). Linking career counseling to personality disorders. In R. Feller & G. Walz (Eds.), *Career transitions inturbulent times: Exploring work, learning and careers*. Greenboro, NC: Eric Clearinghouse on Counseling and Student Services. (ERIC Document Reproduction No. ED398519)

Kneishok, T., Ulneir, J., Hecox, J., & Welterstein, K. (2000). Resume therapy and vocational test feedback: Tailoring interventions to self-efficacy outcomes. *Journal of Career Assessment and Self-Efficacy 8*(3), 267-81.

Krumboltz, J. D. (1983). *Private rules in career decision-making*. Special publication series No. 38. Columbus, OH: National Center for Research in Vocational Education.

Krumboltz, J. D. (1996). A learning theory of career counseling. In M. L Savickas & W. B. Walsh (Eds.), *Handbook of career counseling and practice* (pp. 55-81). Palo Alto, CA: Davies-Black.

Krumboltz, J. D., & Hamel, D. A. (1977). *Guide to career decision-making skills*. New York: Educational Testing Service.

Krumboltz, J. D., Mitchell, A., & Gelatt, H. G. (1975). Application of social learning theory of career selection. *Focus on Guidance, 8*, 1-16.

Krumboltz, J. D., & Nichols, C. (1990). Integrating the social learning theory of career decision-making. In W. B. Walsh & S. H. Osipow (Eds.), *Career counseling: Contemporary topics in vocational psychology* (pp. 159-192). Hillsdale, NJ: Erlbaum.

Kuhn, D. (1989). Children and adults as intuitive scientists. *Psychological Review, 96*, 674-698.

Kummerow, J. (2000). *New directions in career planning and the workplace* (2nd ed.). Palo Alto, CA: Davies-Black.

Lapan, R. T., Boggs, K. R., & Morrill, W. H. (1989). Self-efficacy as a mediator of investigative and realistic general occupational themes on the Strong-Campbell Interest Inventory. *Journal of Counseling Psychology, 3*(6), 176-288.

Lent, R. W., Hatckett, G., & Brown, S. D. (1996). Social cognitive framework for studying career choice and transition to work. *Journal of Vocational Education Research 21*(4), 3-31.

Lent, R. W., Larkin, K. C., & Brown, S. D. (1989). Relation of self-efficacy to inventoried vocational interests. *Journal of Vocational Behavior, 34*, 176-182.

Leong, F. T. L. (Eds.). (1995). *Career development and vocational behavior of racial and ethnic minorities*. Mahwah, NJ: Erlbaum.

Leung, A. S. (1995). Career development and counseling: A multicultural perspective. In J. Ponterotto, J. M. Casas, L. A. Suzuki, & C. M. Alexander (Eds.), *Handbook of multicultural counseling* (pp. 549-566). Thousand Oaks, CA: Sage.

Litak, C. K. (1989). Getting down to cases: Career re-evaluation: The case of Justin. *Career Development Quarterly, 37*, 295-297.

Lopez, F. (1989). Current family dynamics, trait anxiety, and academic adjustment: Test of a family-based model of vocational identity. *Journal of Vocational Behavior, 35*, 76-87.

Marcia, J. (1966). Development and validation of ego identity status. *Journal of Personality and Social Psychology, 3*, 551-558.

McBride, P. (2001). *Career counseling with minorities in the new millennium: Turning promise into practice*. Retrieved from http://icdl.uncg.edu/sc/mcbride1.html

McDaniels, C. A. (2000, June). *Words from the wise*. Paper presented at the National Career Development Association Conference, Pittsburgh, PA. (Available at ERIC/CASS International Career Development Library)

Mitchell, K., & Levin, A. S., & Krumboltz, J. D. (1999). Planned happenstance: Constructing unexpected career opportunities. *Journal of Counseling and Development, 77*, 115-124.

Mitchell, L. K., & Krumboltz, J. D. (1990). Social learning approach to career decision making: Krumboltz's theory. In D. Brown & L. Brooks (Eds.), *Career choice & development* (2nd ed., pp. 145-196). San Francisco: Jossey-Bass.

Mitchell, L. K., & Krumboltz, J. D. (1996). Learning theory of career choice and counseling. In D. Brown & L. Brooks (Eds.), *Career choice and development* (3rd ed., pp. 233-276). San Fransisco: Jossey-Bass.

Montana, P. J. (1989). Career development in our nation's business schools. A survey report on policies and practices, plus a career course syllabus currently in use. *Journal of Career Planning and Placement, 49*, 61-64.

Moses, N. C. (1989). Coping with fear of failure: The case of Justin. *Career Development Quarterly, 37*, 302-305.

National Research Center for Career and Technical Education. (2001). *A taxonomy of career development interventions that occur in U.S. secondary schools*. National Dissemination Center for Career and Technical Education. The Ohio State University

Newman, J. L., Fuqua, D. R., & Seaworth, T. B. (1989). The role of anxiety in career indecision: Implications for diagnosis and treatment. *Career Development Quarterly, 37*, 221-231.

Neimeyer, G. J., Brown, M. T., Metzler, A. E., Hagans, C., & Tangum, M. (1989). The impact of sex, sex-role orientation, and construct type on vocational differential, integration and conflict. *Journal of Vocational Behavior, 34,* 236-251.

Niles, S. G. (1989). The influence of life roles and readiness for career decision-making: The case of Fabian: *Career Development Quarterly, 38,* 28-32.

Occupational Outlook Handbook. (2001-2001). *Bureau of Statistics: Bulletin 2540-1.* Washington, DC: U.S. Department of Labor

Oliver, L. W., & Spokane, A. R. (1988). Career-intervention outcomes: What contributes to client gain? *Journal of Counseling Psychology, 35,* 447-462.

Olson, C., McWhirter, E., & Horan, J. J. (1989). A decision-making model applied to career counseling. *Journal of Career Development, 16,* 107-117.

Osipow, S. H. (1989). *Manual career decision scale.* Odessa, FL: Psychological Assessment Resources.

Pallas, A M., Natriello, G., & McDill, E. L. (1989). The changing nature of the disadvantaged population: Current dimensions and future trends. *Journal of Career Development, 18*(5), 16-22.

Peavy, R. V. (1994). A constructivist perspective for counseling. *Educational and Vocational Guidance Bulletin, 55,* 341-37.

Peterson, G., Long, K., & Bippuos, A. (1999). The effects of three career interventions on educational choices of eighth grade students. *Professional School Counseling, 3*(1), 34-42.

Petridor, E., & Spathes, C. (2001). Designing training interventions: Human & technical training. *International Journal of Training and Development, 5*(3), 185-95.

Pope, M. (1995). Career interventions for gay and lesbian clients: A synopsis of practice knowledge an research needs. *Career Development Quarterly, 44*(2), 191-203.

Prideaux, L., Creed, P., Muller, J., & Patton, W. (2000). A review of career intervention from an educational perspective. Have investigations shed any light? *Swiss Journal of Psychology, 59*(4), *221-226.*

Raskin, P. M. (1989). Identity status research: Implications for career counseling. Journal of Adolescence, *12,* 375-388.

Reardon, R. C. (1996). A program and cost analysis of a self-directed career decision making program in a university career center. *Journal of Counseling and Development, 74,* 280-285.

Rifkin, J. (1995). *The end of work—Technology, jobs, and your future.* New York: Putnam.

Robinson, T. L., & Howard-Hamilton, M. F. (2000). *The convergence of race, ethnicity, and gender—Multiple identities in counseling.* Upper Saddle River, NJ: Merrill-Prentice Hall.

Rodriguez, L. M., & Blocker, D. (1988). A comparison of two approaches to enhancing career maturity in Puerto Rican college women. *Journal of Counseling Psychology, 35,* 273-280.

Rounds, J. B., & Tinsley, H. E. A. (1984). Diagnosis and treatment of vocational problems. In S. Brown & R. Lent (Eds.), *Handbook of counseling psychology* (pp. 137-177). New York: Wiley.

Rounds, J. B., & Tracey, T. J. (1990). From trait-and-factor to person-environment-fit counseling: Theory and process. In W. B. Walsh & S. J. Osipow (Eds.), *Career counseling: Contemporary topics in vocational psychology* (pp. 1-44). Hilldale, NJ: Erlbaum.

Sampson, J. P., Jr. (1989). Introduction. In G. R. Walz & J. C. Bleuer (Eds.), *Counseling intervention strategies for computer-assisted career guidance: An important-processing approach* (pp. 139-154). Pacific Grove, CA: Brooks/Cole.

Sampson, J. P., Peterson, G. W., Reardon, R. C., & Lenz, J. G. (2000). Using readiness assessment to improve career services: A cognitive information processing approach. *Career Development Quarterly, 49,* 146-174.

Sampson, J. P., Readon, R. C., Peterson, G., & Lenz, J. (2003). *Career counseling and services: A cognitive information processing approach.* Florida State University:

Savickas, M. L. (1989a). Annual review: Practice and research in career counseling and development, 1988. *Career Development Quarterly, 38,* 100-134.

Savickas, M. L. (1989b). Career-style assessment and counseling. In T. Sweeney (Ed.), *Adlerian counseling: A practical approach for a new decade* (3rd ed., pp. 289-320). Municie, IN: Accelerated Development.

Savickas, M. L. (1997). The spirit in career counseling: Fostering self-completion through work. In D. Bloch & L. Richmond (Eds.), *Connections between spirit and work in career development* (pp. 3-25). Palo Alto, CA: Black/Davies.

Schlossberg, N. K., Waters, E. B., & Goodman, J. (1995). *Counseling adults in transition: Linking practice with theory* (2nd ed.). New York: Springer.

School Safety Center. (1986). Increasing Student Attendance. (NSSC Resource Paper). Sacramento, CA. (ERIC Document Reproduction Service No. ED273 045)

Sexton, T. L., Whiston, C. S., Bleuer, J. C., & Walz, G. R. (1997). *Integrating outcome research into counseling practice and training.* Alexandria, VA: American Counseling Association.

Skovholt, T. M., Morgan, J. I., & Negron-Cunningham, N. (1989). Mental imagery in career counseling and life planning: A review of research and intervention models. *Journal of Counseling and Development, 67,* 287-292.

Smart, J. C. (1989). Life history influences on Holland vocational type development. *Journal of Vocational Behavior, 34,* 69-87.

Solly, D. C. (1987). A career development model for the mentally handicapped: Techniques: *Remedial Education and Counseling, 3,* 294-300.

Spokane, A. R. (1989). Are there psychological and mental health consequences of difficult career decisions: *Journal of Career Development, 16,* 19-23.

Spokane, A. R., & Hawks, B. K. (1990). Annual review: Practice and research in career counseling and development, 1989. *Career Development Quarterly, 39,* 98-129.

Spokane, A. R., & Oliver, L. W. (1983). The outcomes of vocational interventions. In S. H. Osipow & W. B. Walsh (Eds.), *Handbook of vocational psychology* (Vol. 2, pp. 99-116). Hillsdale, NJ: Erlbaum.

Stewart, R. A. (1989). The use of computers in career planning, placement, and recruit. *Journal of Career Planning and Placement, 49,* 51-53.

Subich, L. M. (1989). A challenge to grow: Reaction to Hoyt's article. *Career Development Quarterly, 37,* 213-217.

Sue, D. W., & Sue, D. (1999). *Counseling the culturally different* (3rd ed.). New York: John Wiley & Sons.

Super, D. E. (1957). *The psychology of careers*. New York: Harper & Row.

Super, D. E. (1990). A life-span, life-space approach to career development. In D. Brown, L. Brook, & Associates (Eds.), *Career choice and development: Applying contemporary theories to practice* (2nd ed., pp. 197-261). San Francisco: Josey-Bass.

Swanson, J. L. (1996). The theory is the practice: Trait-and-factor/person-environment. In M. L. Savickas & W. B. Walsh (Eds.), *Handbook for career counseling theory and practice* (p. 93). Palo Alto, CA: Davies-Black.

Szapocznik, J., Rio, A., Murray, E., Cohen, R., Scopetta, M., Rivas-Vasquez, A., Hervis, O., Posada, V., & Durtines, W. (1989). Structural family versus psychodynamic child therapy for problematic Hispanic boys. *Journal of Consulting and Clinical Psychology, 57,* 571-578.

Szymanski, E. M., & Hanley-Maxwell, C. (1996). Career development for people with developmental disabilities: An ecological model. *Journal of Rehabilitation, 64,* 48-55.

Tennyson, W. W., Miller, G. D., Skovholt, T. M., & Williams, R. C. (1989). How they view their role: A survey of counselors in different secondary schools. *Journal of Counseling and Development, 67,* 399-403.

Toman, S. (1989). Getting down to cases: Issues of a non-traditional student: The case of Fabian. *Career Development Quarterly, 38,* 25-27.

Valentine, E. (1998). *Gender differences in learning and achievement in mathematics, science and technology and strategies for equality: A literature review.* Blacksburg, VA: Polytechnic Institute and State University. (ERIC Document Reproduction Service No. ED416915)

Walz, G. R., & Bleuer, J. C. (Eds). (1989). *Counseling software guide.* Alexandria, VA: American Association for Counseling and Development.

Waters, E. B., & Goodman, J. (1990). *Empowering older adults—Practical strategies for counselors.* San Francisco: Jossey-Bass.

Wehrly, B., & Kenney, K. R., & Kenney, M. E. (1999). *Counseling multiracial families.* Thousand Oaks, CA: Sage.

Wolleat, P. L. (1989). Reconciling sex differences in information-processing and career outcomes. *Journal of Career Development, 16,* 97-106.

Wonacott, M. (2001). *Secondary career development interventions:* In Brief Fast Facts for Policy and Practice, No. 13. National Dissemination Center for Career and Technical Education. Columbus. OH: Office of Vocational and Adult Education, Washington, DC. (ERIC Document Reproduction Service No. ED 452375)

Worell, J., & Etaugh, C. (1994). Transforming theory and research with women: Themes and variations (Special Issue). *Psychology of Women Quarterly, 18*(4).

Yalom, I. D. (1989). *Love's executioner: And other tales of psychotherapy.* New York: Basic Books.

Zunker, V. (2002). *Career counseling: Applied concepts of life planning.* Pacific Grove, CA: Brooks/Cole.

CHAPTER 6

THE IMPACT OF PARENT-ADOLESCENT RELATIONSHIPS ON ADULT CAREER CHOICES

Briana K. Keller and Susan C. Whiston

The purpose of the following study is to examine the association between parent-adolescent relationships, gender, and adult career choices. The current study utilizes parent-adolescent relationship data gathered from the children at age 18 and occupational choice information gathered from the children at age 23. The data were taken from the Intergenerational Study of Parents and Children (Thornton & Freeman, 1998) which is a 32-year longitudinal study of parents and their children. The results suggest that parents may not influence their adolescent offspring's career choice to the degree previously indicated. In addition, this study did not find differences among males and females in parent-adolescent relationships and career choice.

It has become increasingly clearer over the past 50 years that the environment plays a large role in career development (Holland, 1992; Mitchell & Krumboltz, 1996). One salient component of an individual's environment is his/her family. Researchers and practitioners in a variety of fields such

Issues in Career Development, 129–145

as counseling psychology, secondary education, and higher education have wondered about the interface between various family and career variables since Roe theorized that parental styles had a significant influence on individuals' career direction in 1956. Interest in this topic increased in the 1980s when family systems theorists proposed that career decision-making is affected by the family system (Bratcher, 1982). According to family systems theory, the family operates as a system or unit, where patterns of interactions evolve and relational aspects of the system have a significant influence on individuals' behavior (Carr, 2000). The proposed impact of the family system on individuals' career development was extended by Zingaro (1983), who theorized that clients may have difficulty making career decisions due to a low level of differentiation from the nuclear family and that these clients may not be able to differentiate their own career expectations from their parents' expectations. Family systems theory continues to impact career development theory and practice, as many studies have been conducted in an attempt to illuminate the precise ways in which the family of origin influences career-related issues. The results tend to support the idea that family variables and career variables are related (Whiston & Keller, 2004).

One career variable that has been of interest for many years is career choice. In other words, researchers have tried for many years to understand the factors that influence one's decision regarding what field of work to pursue. The family of origin is one specific factor that has been of interest to researchers over the past 50 years. The results of several studies indicate that one's career choice is influenced by various aspects of his/her family of origin. For example, Nachmann (1960) found that maternal employment was related to career choice. More recently, Trice (1991) found that paternal occupation was related to adults' occupational choices. Paternal occupation was also found to be salient in a study by Johnson et al. (1983). More specifically, the researchers found that father's occupational status, as well as both parents' educational statuses, were positively correlated with occupational attainment for Americans of European and Japanese ancestry.

In addition to examining family influences on general occupational choices, researchers have examined family influences on specific aspects of career choice, such as traditionality and prestige. For example, the traditionality of women's career choices tends to be related to identification with and emotional support from their parents (Lunneborg, 1982), parental involvement and pride (Standley & Soule, 1974), maternal education and fathers' favorable attitudes towards mothers working (Bielby, 1978). Additionally, parental socioeconomic status and autonomous-relatedness behaviors within the family have been shown to be related to adults' occupational prestige (Bell, Allen, Hauser, & O'Connor, 1996).

One of the more prevalent findings in the empirical literature is that familial relationships greatly impact career choice and various aspects thereof. This trend corroborates the basic tenet of family systems theory; that relational aspects of the family system have a significant influence on individuals' behavior (Carr, 2000). For instance, Nachmann (1960) found that parent-child relationships were related to career choice, while Bell, Allen, Hauser, and O'Connor (1996) found that the degree of autonomy support provided by both parents was associated with the level of prestige of adults' career choices. Other studies have specifically examined family relational influences on the gender traditionality of women's career choices. Tangri (1972) found that college-aged women planning to enter nontraditional careers reported cognitive distance from both parents, warm feelings toward their mother, and perceived similarity to their father. Trigg and Perlman (1976) found that women following nontraditional career paths had parents who supported their desire to enter nontraditional careers. Their finding was supported by O'Donnell and Andersen (1978), who found that only 30% of women participants in traditional majors indicated that their parents expected them to work after college, while 80% of the women in nontraditional careers indicated this was true. Similarly, Houser and Garvey (1983) found that 60% of the women in nontraditional careers said their parents encouraged them to pursue a nontraditional career, whereas only 19% of those in traditional careers stated the same.

The attitudes of fathers and other male role models also seem to have a significant influence on women's tendency to enter a nontraditional field. For instance, Houser and Garvey (1983) concluded that women in nontraditional careers received more support from father and brother(s), regarding pursuit of a nontraditional career than women who were in traditional careers. Additionally, Hackett, Esposito, and O'Halloran (1989) found that positive paternal influences were strongly predictive of college women's consideration of nontraditional occupations.

As illustrated, many studies conducted over the past 40 years suggest that family factors, particularly family relationships, influence career direction. In fact, Jacobsen (1971) found that 92% of fathers and 80% of mothers felt they had tried to promote their son's interest in specific careers. The purpose of the following study is to investigate the more subtle family relational influences and whether they impact actual career choices, thereby further elucidating the nature of the association between family relationships and career direction. However, the current study differs from and improves on the aforementioned studies in several important ways. First, the current study differs from all previously mentioned studies, except Nachmann (1960), in that it seeks to examine how family relationships influence the occupational group into which one's occupation fits, rather than the traditionality or prestige of one's career choice. More specifically, the current study seeks to understand whether or not familial relationships influence individuals' decisions to pursue a career in social work over science, welding over art, bookkeeping over business, and so forth. In other words, the current study seeks to understand if family relationships impact membership in occupational groups.

On a similar note, this study differs from that of Nachmann (1960) by using recent theory to group occupations into broad categories and by examining a wide variety of career choices rather than just dentistry, social work, and law. More specifically, the current study examines family influences on career choice by grouping occupations into six empirically supported categories according to the theory of John L. Holland (1994), a well-known career development theorist. The third way in which the current study differs from previous studies regarding family influences on career choice is that it seeks to illuminate family relational influences on the career choices of both males and females, as opposed to studying just males (Nachmann, 1960) or females (Hackett, Esposito, & O'Halloran, 1989; Houser & Garvey, 1983; O'Donnell & Andersen, 1978; Tangri, 1972; Trigg & Perlman, 1976).

The final way in which the current study differs from and improves on the other studies that have examined the association between family relationships and career choice is that the current study seeks to examine the long-term effects of one's family relationships on career choice, rather than the immediate effects. While most studies have examined the impact of family relationships on *current* career choice, this study examines how one's relationships with family members at one point in time impact his/her career choice 5 years later. In other words, the longitudinal nature of this study answers several researchers' calls (Vondracek, Lerner, & Schulenberg, 1986) for more longitudinal research in this area and fills a significant void in this area of research, thus moving the understanding of the association between family issues and career issues to a new level.

To summarize, the current study seeks to elucidate the nature of the association between relationships within one's family of origin and the occupational field he/she chooses to pursue. The current study strives to answer the following questions: (a) Does the nature of the relationship one has with his/her mother at age 18 influence the occupational group in which he/she is engaged at age 23?, (b) Is this association significantly different for males and females?, (c) Does the nature of the relationship one has with his/her father at age 18 influence the occupational group in which he/she is engaged at age 23?, and (d) Is this association significantly different for males and females?

METHODS

Data Source

The data for this study are taken from the Intergenerational Study of Parents and Children conducted by Arland Thornton and Deborah Freedman (1998) and made available by the InterUniversity Consortium for Political and Social Research. The study was designed to examine the causes and consequences of family formation and dissolution among young adults over a 32-year period. Data were collected on 1,113 individuals born in the Detroit area in 1961. Interviews were conducted with the mothers of these individuals twice in 1962, and once each in 1963, 1966, 1977, 1980, 1985, and 1993. The individuals who were born in 1961 were interviewed in 1980, 1985, and 1993. In addition to the interviews, data regarding major events in the children's lives were collected through the use of life history calendars.

The data used in this particular study were taken from two waves of data collection in the Intergenerational Study of Parents and Children: 1980 and 1985. More specifically, the current study utilizes data gathered from the children at ages 18 and 23 years. The data were collected through personal interviews and surveys in both 1980 and 1985. At these times, the participants were asked dozens of questions about their views regarding family life, occupational and educational expectations and attainment, relationships with their parents, perceptions of their parents' willingness to be of assistance to them, and views about themselves.

Sample

The current sample was drawn from a total of 923 individuals still participating in the Intergenerational Study of Parents and Children in 1985. These individuals were all born to Caucasian couples in the Detroit metropolitan area in 1961. Approximately equal numbers of the participants were first, second, and fourth born children; data were not collected on individuals born in 1961 who were third born children. While the participants all lived in Detroit at the beginning of the study in 1961, they were spread across more than 20 states at the time of the 1985 data collection wave. The attrition rate from 1961 to 1980 was 16%, while the total attrition rate from 1961 to 1985 was 17.1%.

A number of participants ($n = 369$) were eliminated from the final analyses due to insufficient data. The majority of these individuals were eliminated because they did not answer the family relationship questions regarding their natural born parents, which could have confounded the results ($n = 99$), or because they had not received any type of vocational or academic training following high school, thus making it impossible to determine their occupational choice ($n = 164$). Thus, there were 271 males and 282 females represented in the data analyses for a total sample size of 553.

Measures

Parent-adolescent relationships. Information regarding the participants' relationships with their mothers and fathers was ascertained in 1980, at which time the researchers asked the participants seven questions about the relationship with each of their natural parents. The questions were written in Likert scale format with *1 = Always, 2 = Usually, 3 = Sometimes,* and *4 = Never.* The seven questions are as follows: (a) My mother's/ father's ideas and opinions about the important things in life are ones I can respect, (b) My mother/father respects my opinions about the important things in life, (c) My mother/father accepts me and understands me as a person, (d) I enjoy doing things together with my mother/father, (e) My mother/father makes it easy for me to confide in her/him, (f) My mother/father gives me the right amount of affection, and (g) When something is bothering me, I am able to talk it over with my mother/ father.

Occupational choice. For purposes of the current study, occupational choice is represented by the major area of study associated with the college degree or noncollege training obtained by participants. While this is an imperfect measure of occupational choice, occupational choice is often represented by college major in this area of research (Switzer, Grigg, Miller, & Young, 1962; Trigg & Perlman, 1976; Weishaar, Green, & Craighead, 1981). Information regarding occupational group was ascertained in 1985, at which time the researchers asked the participants about the educational training they had received since their interview in 1980, around the time of their high school graduation. More specifically, participants who had received any type of college degree (associate's, bachelor's, master's, etc.) were asked to indicate the major or majors associated with each degree, while participants who had not earned college degrees but had participated in some type of training (vocational school, certificate program, nondegree college work, etc.) were asked to indicate the major associated with each type of training. The researchers assigned two-digit codes to the majors indicated, which corresponded to a master list of occupational codes constructed by the researchers in the original study.

For individuals who indicated two majors for a particular degree, the second major listed was used because it was presumed to be the major associated with the actual completion of their degree. For individuals who had received more than one degree, the occupational code from their most recently received degree was used because it presumably is the most indicative of their career choice. For individuals who had received a degree and another type of training, the occupational code from their degree was used because the expenditure of energy, time, and money associated with earning a college degree indicates a higher level of commitment to a specific occupational area than participation in other types of training. Lastly, individuals who had not received a degree, but had received more than one type of training were eliminated because it was impossible to determine which training was most indicative of their career choice.

There were 99 occupational codes included in the master occupational list. As making sense of a dependent variable with 99 levels would be very difficult, the occupational codes needed to be grouped in some way. A common way to classify occupations is to use codes based on the work of John L. Holland (1994) and his associates. According to Holland's system, there are six major categories of occupations (realistic, investigative, artistic, social, enterprising, and conventional; RIASEC) which vary along several dimensions such as requirements, rewards, values, and tasks. Each occupation has a 3-letter code that indicates the three categories in which they most closely fit, with the first letter representing the category of best fit (Holland, 1994).

Holland's classification system was used in this study as a way to condense the 99 possible occupations into more manageable units of analysis. Hence, each occupation included on the master occupational list was located in *The Educational Opportunities Finder* (Rosen, Holmberg, & Holland, 1994) and the first letter of the Holland code associated with each occupation was recorded. Then the majors associated with the participants' college degrees and nondegree training were assigned a 1-letter Holland code. Individuals who responded to the question regarding majors by answering *other specific major* were eliminated because it was impossible to assign a Holland code to them.

Analyses

The first two research questions were tested two ways. First, the answers to the seven questions regarding the adolescents' relationships with their mothers were summed into a total mother relationship score. A two-way analysis of variance (ANOVA) was conducted to evaluate the association between occupational group, gender, and the total mother relationship score. The occupational group main effect and occupational group X gen-

Table 6.1.   Factor Loadings

	Respect	Closeness
Respect items		
1. My parent's ideas & opinions about the important things in life are ones I can respect.	.82	.34
2. My parent respects my opinion about the important things in life.	.88	.33
3. My parent accepts me and understands me as a person.	.81	.38
Closeness items		
4. My parent makes it easy for me to confide in him/her.	.37	.86
5. My parent gives me the right amount of affection.	.44	.73
6. When something is bothering me, I am able to talk it over with my parent.	.30	.88
Complexly determined item		
7. I enjoy doing things with my parent.	.63	.58

der interaction effect were of interest. An alpha level of .05 was considered significant.

The aforementioned statistical procedure assumes the seven relationship questions all hang together as a single construct. However, it was speculated that the seven questions might cluster into more than one factor within the relationship construct. Therefore, three principal components factor analyses—one with just the mother data, one with just the father data, and one with the mother and father data combined—were conducted. In each of the factor analyses, the eigenvalues and scree tests indicated that the relationship construct contained two factors. Thus, two factors were rotated using a Varimax rotation procedure. The rotated solution from the analysis including both mother and father data is shown in Table 6.1. As shown, three relationship questions loaded highly on the first factor (respect), three relationship questions loaded highly on the second factor (closeness), and one question loaded on both factors approximately equally and was discarded. The coefficient alpha for each factor was .80. The respect factor accounted for 30.0% of the variance while the closeness factor accounted for 29.1% of the variance.

Because it is likely that the two dependent variables, the respect and closeness factors, are related, the multivariate analysis of variance (MANOVA) technique was chosen. More specifically, a two-way MANOVA was conducted to determine the association between occupational group, gender, and the respect and closeness scores. The occupational group main effect and occupational group X gender interaction effect were of interest. An alpha level of .05 was considered significant. The final two research questions (regarding fathers) were tested using methods identical to the ones used to test the first two questions.

RESULTS

The first research question asks whether or not the nature of the relationship one has with his/her mother at age 18 influences the occupational group in which he/she is engaged at age 23. The results of the two-way ANOVA between occupational group, gender, and the total mother-adolescent relationship score indicated no significant main effect for occupational group, $F(5, 541) = .302$, $p = .912$. The means and standard deviations for total mother-adolescent relationship scores as a function of occupational group are presented in Table 6.2. The results of the two-way MANOVA between occupational group, gender, and the mother respect and closeness factors indicated no significant main effect for occupational group, Wilks' $\lambda = .981$, $F(10, 1080) = 1.015$, $p = .428$. The means and standard deviations are presented in Table 6.2. In summary, the results suggest that there is no association between occupational group and mother-adolescent relationships.

The second question of interest is whether or not the association between adolescent-mother relationships and adult career choices is significantly different for males and females. The results of the two-way ANOVA between occupational group, gender, and the total mother-adolescent relationship score indicated no significant interaction effect between occupational group and gender, $F(5, 541) = 1.32$, $p = .253$. Likewise, the results of the two-way MANOVA indicated no significant interaction effect between occupational group, gender, and the mother Respect and Closeness factors, Wilks' $\lambda = .975$, $F(10, 1080) = 1.394$, $p = .178$. The means and standard deviations for the total mother-adolescent relationship scores, the respect factor, and the closeness factor as a function of occupational group and gender are presented in Table 6.2. In summary, the results suggest that the association between occupational groups and mother-adolescent relationships does not vary as a function of gender.

While the first two research questions concern maternal influences, the following two questions address the ways in which fathers influence their children's career choices. More specifically, the third research question asks whether or not the relationship one has with his/her father at age 18 influences the occupational group in which he/she is engaged at age 23. The results of the two-way ANOVA between occupational group, gender,

**Table 6.2.   Means and Standard Deviations Regarding the
Association between Occupational Group, Gender, and
Mother-Adolescent Relationship Scores**

Occupational Group		Total Mother		Respect		Closeness	
		M	SD	M	SD	M	SD
Realistic	M (n = 128)	15.63	5.97	6.46	2.67	6.82	2.82
	F (n = 14)	13.64	4.57	5.57	1.87	6.29	2.55
	Total (n = 142)	15.44	5.87	6.37	2.61	6.77	2.79
Investigative	M (n = 31)	13.58	4.18	5.71	1.81	5.97	2.11
	F (n = 33)	14.24	4.61	5.82	1.93	6.52	2.48
	Total (n = 64)	13.92	4.38	5.77	1.86	6.25	2.30
Artistic	M (n = 22)	16.77	12.42	7.41	6.57	6.68	4.84
	F (n = 29)	12.79	4.01	5.24	1.72	5.76	2.08
	Total (n = 51)	14.51	8.82	6.18	4.58	6.16	3.53
Social	M (n = 34)	14.53	4.24	5.85	1.91	6.38	2.20
	F (n = 103)	13.50	6.32	5.80	2.84	5.97	2.92
	Total (n =137)	13.76	5.88	5.81	2.63	6.07	2.75
Enterprising	M (n = 40)	14.00	3.82	5.43	1.58	6.45	2.12
	F (n = 55)	13.75	4.68	5.64	1.91	6.31	2.49
	Total (n = 95)	13.85	4.32	5.55	1.77	6.37	2.33
Conventional	M (n = 16)	14.13	3.28	6.00	1.21	6.06	1.84
	F (n = 48)	14.77	4.60	6.62	1.99	6.56	2.34
	Total (n =64)	14.61	4.30	6.13	1.82	6.44	2.22

and the total father-adolescent relationship score indicated no significant main effect for occupational group, $F(5, 541) = 1.20$, $p = .310$. Similarly, the results of the two-way MANOVA between occupational group, gender, and the father respect and closeness factors revealed no significant main effects for occupational group, Wilks' $\lambda = .972$, $F(10, 1080) = 1.555$, $p = .115$. The means and standard deviations associated with these analyses are presented in Table 3. In summary, the results suggest that there is no association between occupational group and father-adolescent relationships.

The last question asks whether or not the association between adolescent-father relationships and adult career choices significantly differs for males and females. The results of the two-way ANOVA between occupational group, gender, and the total father-adolescent relationship score indicated no significant interaction effect between occupational group and gender, $F(5, 541) = 1.26$, $p = .281$. Likewise, the results of the two-way MANOVA indicated no significant interaction effect between occupational group, gender, and the father respect and closeness factors, Wilks' $\lambda = .973$, $F(10, 1080) = 1.496$, $p = .135$. The means and standard devia-

Table 6.3.   Means and Standard Deviations Regarding the Association between Occupational Group, Gender, and Father-Adolescent Relationship Scores

Occupational Group		Total Father		Respect		Closeness	
		M	SD	M	SD	M	SD
Realistic	M (n = 128)	15.74	6.51	6.33	2.80	7.30	3.02
	F (n = 14)	19.14	14.08	7.93	6.03	8.71	6.13
	Total (n = 142)	16.08	7.58	6.49	3.26	7.44	3.45
Investigative	M (n = 31)	15.65	4.05	6.29	1.74	7.45	2.01
	F (n = 33)	17.70	9.88	6.97	4.36	8.42	4.26
	Total (n = 64)	16.70	7.65	6.64	3.35	7.95	3.38
Artistic	M (n = 22)	17.0	11.77	7.59	5.88	7.23	4.99
	F (n = 29)	15.45	4.03	6.0	1.69	7.45	2.01
	Total (n = 51)	16.12	8.24	6.69	4.09	7.35	3.57
Social	M (n = 34)	16.35	5.01	6.65	2.14	7.56	2.68
	F (n = 103)	15.49	4.95	6.13	2.05	7.38	2.56
	Total (n = 137)	15.70	4.96	6.26	2.08	7.42	2.58
Enterprising	M (n = 40)	14.53	3.80	5.68	2.13	7.05	1.96
	F (n = 55)	15.42	5.37	5.95	2.41	7.69	3.51
	Total (n = 95)	15.04	4.77	5.83	2.29	7.42	2.96
Conventional	M (n = 16)	15.06	3.71	6.44	1.55	6.81	1.87
	F (n = 48)	16.31	4.79	6.29	1.99	7.79	2.48
	Total (n = 64)	16.00	4.55	6.33	1.88	7.55	2.36

tions for these analyses are presented in Table 6.3. In summary, the results suggest that the association between occupational groups and father-adolescent relationships do not vary as a function of gender.

Supplemental Analyses

The lack of significant findings in the primary analyses led to the conclusion that perhaps another variable or set of variables was moderating the association between the family relationship variables and career choice. In particular, it was hypothesized that parents' income may have affected the adolescents' educational opportunities, which in turn, was related to occupational choice, especially since the current study utilizes college/training major to represent occupational choice. Therefore, information regarding total family income was ascertained from the data gathered from the mothers in 1980 and supplemental analyses were conducted for each dependent variable (total relationship, respect, and closeness scores for both mother and father) using family income as a covariate. The relationship between family income and the father close-ness factor, controlling for occupational choice, was significant $F(1, 533)$ $= 4.67, p = .031$. However, the relationship between family income and the other five dependent variables was not significant. Thus, it was con-cluded that family income was not significantly moderating the associa-tion between family relationships and career choice in the current data.

DISCUSSION

According to family systems theory, relationships and interactions within the family system affect career development (Bratcher, 1982; Zingaro, 1983). Therefore, in the current study, it was hypothesized that parent-adolescent relationships would impact adults' occupational choices. The results of the current study, however, did not support this hypothesis. More specifically, the results did not support the idea that mother-adoles-cent relationships and father-adolescent relationships influence the type of career one decides to pursue, as measured by the Holland code associ-ated with one's most recent degree or training. These results are in con-trast to findings from other studies which have indicated that one's relationships with his/her parents influence his/her career choices (Nach-mann, 1960) and various aspects thereof such as traditionality (Hackett, Esposito, & O'Halloran, 1989; Houser & Garvey, 1983; Tangri, 1972; Trigg & Perlman, 1976) and prestige (Bell, Allen, Hauser, & O'Connor, 1996).

The results from the current study could differ from the results of pre-vious studies for three major reasons. First, while the current study exam-ined longitudinal family influences, the majority of the other studies in this area examined immediate family influences. Perhaps parent-adoles-cent relationships exert significant influence during adolescence but less influence as the adolescents mature into young adults. The second possi-ble reason explaining why the current results are in contrast to the find-ings from other studies is that the construct of relationships was measured differently in the various studies. In several of the previous studies (Hack-ett, Esposito, & O'Halloran, 1989; Houser & Garvey, 1983), the relation-ship questions tapped parental behaviors and attitudes specifically towards career issues, whereas the questions in the current study tapped more general relational aspects. Perhaps the ways in which parents inter-act with their children regarding career and educational issues are more influential than the ways in which they interact with them on day-to-day issues. The final possible reason the current results contradict the results from previous studies is that participants in this study were engaged in a variety of educational and occupational activities at the time of the second data collection, while participants in previous studies were all enrolled in some type of post-secondary education at the time of data collection. Perhaps parental influences differ between a group of individuals pursuing university training and a group of individuals with mixed educational and occupational situations. This discrepancy underscores the need for researchers to refrain from using convenient college samples. The results from studies using such samples may not generalize to other samples.

Despite its dearth of significant findings, the current study makes an important contribution to the collection of literature regarding the impact of family of origin issues on career development variables in several ways. First, the current study looked at a specific career development variable and a specific family variable in isolation. While this fact could be considered by some to be a limitation, this is important because the nature of the association between family of origin issues and career development issues is extremely complex, and hence, empirical research that teases apart the many variables encompassed by these constructs can help foster a more exact understanding of the nature of the association between these two constructs. The fact that no association was found among basic family relational variables such as respect and closeness and occupational choice may indicate that the influence of family relationships on occupational choice may have been overestimated in previous research.

The second way in which the current study contributes to the literature is by using longitudinal data rather than cross-sectional data. Perhaps the reason the current study failed to find significant associations between family relationships and career choice while other studies have found significant associations between these constructs is because the effects of family relationships on career choice are temporary and short-lived, while this study looked at the long-term effects. This study can help clarify the differential impact of family of origin issues on career variables at different points in time, which is an important contribution to this line of research.

Finally, the current study contributes to the literature regarding the association between parent-adolescent relationships and career choice by using John Holland's established theory. Most of the studies in this general area of inquiry fail to incorporate theory into the methodology, thus making interpretation difficult and comparison across studies nearly impossible. The results of this study, however, could be easily compared with other studies that have examined differences between individuals within Holland's six occupational groups.

While the current study does make a significant contribution to the literature, it has a few limitations that could have affected the results and their generalizability. First, the sample was homogenous regarding ethnicity and geographic location. However, the sample size was still relatively large ($n = 553$) and the sample was diverse regarding other important variables such as socioeconomic status. Second, the manner in which occupational choice was measured (i.e., the major associated with an individual's most recent degree or type of training) is imperfect and perhaps results based on data including information on adults' actual occupations would yield different results. Obtaining actual occupational information for a sample size as large as the one in the current study, however, would be very difficult. Finally, a very small number of questions with a limited response set were used to measure a very large independent construct: parent-adolescent relationships. Perhaps some important aspects of parent-adolescent relationships not tapped by these questions would be associated with occupational choice.

As discussed, the current study is unique from other studies that have looked at the association between family relationships and career choice in several ways. Therefore, despite its limitations, it contributes to the literature in this area in important ways. Yet, there are ample opportunities for the research on the association between family relationships and career choice to be expanded. First, research that defines career choice by the actual occupation in which one is employed, rather than by the major of one's most recent degree or training, is needed. Data of this nature are rare because researchers tend to utilize convenient college samples.

Second, because the results of the current study, as opposed to those of earlier studies, imply that family relationships have different degrees of influence on career choice at different life stages, research that examines career choices of individuals later in life is needed. A few studies have found that the association between family of origin issues and career issues changes over time. For instance, Peterson, Stivers, and Peters (1986) examined the occupational expectations of individuals from fifth grade until approximately age 21 and found that the individuals considered their parents to be the most influential sources regarding their career plans while in fifth and sixth grade as well as in young adulthood but not during late adolescence. Additionally, O'Brien, Friedman, Tipton, and Linn (2000) found that attachment to mother was related to the career self-efficacy scores of female high school students but that attachment to father was the only family variable related to their career self-efficacy scores 5 years later. Perhaps the nature of the association between family relationships and career choice also changes over time. Therefore, research that examines the career choices of individuals at a variety of different ages, especially beyond the college years, could yield interesting results.

The third direction in which the research in this area could expand is the use of different occupational coding schemes. While Holland's system is empirically validated, the categories are very broad. Perhaps studies that use a more specific occupational coding scheme that divides careers into more than six categories would be able to detect fine differences in relationship variables among occupational groups. Finally, there is a need for more comprehensive standardized ways of measuring family relationships. This study used only seven questions, which likely did not capture the complex nature of parent-adolescent relationships. Other studies in this area used standardized measures, such as the Inventory of Parent and Peer Attachment (Armsden & Greenberg, 1987) and the Psychological Separation Inventory (Hoffman, 1984), but these measures capture limited aspects of these relationships as well. Instruments that tap many aspects of parent-adolescent relationships such as the affective, cognitive, behavioral, and spiritual domains are needed. Additionally, because the results of previous studies (Hackett, Esposito, & O'Halloran, 1989; Houser & Garvey, 1983) indicate that family relationships and attitudes specifically regarding career issues may influence career choice more than general family relationships, instruments that assess family relationships and attitudes regarding career issues would be useful.

In conclusion, the results of this longitudinal study indicate that the relationships an individual has with his/her mother and father at age 18 do not significantly influence the specific occupational area associated with his/her career choice 5 years later. This finding contradicts the findings from a number of cross-sectional studies, which indicate that parent-adolescent relationships do impact career choice. Additionally, the results contradict the results of many studies that suggest a variety of family variables impact numerous career variables such as vocational exploration (Felsman & Blustein, 1999), occupational aspirations (Rainey & Borders, 1997), vocational identity (Penick & Jepsen, 1992), and career decision-making (O'Brien, Friedman, Tipton, & Linn, 2000). Therefore, practitioners should continue to consider a variety of family influences when helping clients with career-related concerns, especially when working with adolescent clients. More specifically, counselors should make their clients aware of the potential impact their family of origin may be having on their career development and decision-making processes and explicitly ask them about the ways in which they feel their families could be influencing their current career concerns. This can be especially helpful for clients who seem frustrated or stalled in the career selection process. Through open dialogue about potential family influences, clients will become more aware of the specific ways in which their families are helping and hindering their career development, thus enabling them to construct appropriate ways to capitalize on the positive influences and overcome the negative influences. This will hopefully result in more mature, satisfied, productive workers.

REFERENCES

Armsden, G. C., & Greenberg, M. T. (1987). The inventory of parent and peer attachment: Individual differences and their relationship to psychological well-being in adolescence. *Journal of Youth and Adolescence, 16,* 427-453.

Bell, K. L., Allen, J. P., Hauser, S. T., & O'Connor, T. G. (1996). Family factors and young adult transitions: Educational attainment and occupational prestige. In J. A. Graber, Brooks-Gunn, J., & Petersen, A. C. (Eds.), *Transitions through adolescence: Interpersonal domains and context* (pp. 345-366). Mahwah, NJ: Erlbaum.

Bielby, D. (1978). Maternal employment and socioeconomic status as factors in daughters' career salience: Some substantive refinements. *Sex Roles, 4,* 249-265.

Bratcher, W. E. (1982). The influence of the family on career selection: A family systems perspective. *The Personnel and Guidance Journal, 61,* 87-91.

Carr, A. (2000). *Family therapy: Concepts, process, and practice.* New York: Wiley.

Felsman, D. E., & Blustein, D. L. (1999). The role of peer relatedness in the late adolescent career development. *Journal of Vocational Behavior, 54,* 279-295.

Hackett, G., Esposito, D., & O'Halloran, M. S. (1989). The relationship of role model influences to the career salience and educational and career plans of college women. *Journal of Vocational Behavior, 35,* 164-180.

Hoffman, J. (1984). Psychological separation of late adolescents from their parents. *Journal of Counseling Psychology, 31,* 170-178.

Holland, J. L. (1992). *Making vocational choices* (2nd ed.). Odessa, FL: Psychological Assessment Resources.

Holland, J. L. (1994). *Self-directed search: You and your career.* Odessa, FL: Psychological Assessment Resources.

Houser, B. B., & Garvey, C. (1983). The impact of family, peers, and educational personnel upon career decision making. *Journal of Vocational Behavior, 23,* 35-44.

Jacobsen, R. B. (1971). An exploration of parental encouragement as an intervening variable in occupational–educational learning of children. *Journal of Marriage and the Family, 33,* 174-182.

Johnson, R. C., Nagoshi, C. T., Ahern, F. M., Wilson, J. R., DeFries, J. C., McClearn, G. E., & Vandenberg, S. G. (1983). Family background, cognitive ability, and personality as predictors of educational and occupational attainment. *Social Biology, 30,* 86-100.

Lunneborg, P. W. (1982). Role model influencers of non-traditional professional occupations. *Journal of Vocational Behavior, 20,* 276-281.

Mitchell, L. K., & Krumboltz, J. D. (1996). Krumboltz's learning theory of career choice and counseling. In D. Brown, L. Brooks, & Associates (Eds.), *Career choice and development* (3rd ed., pp. 233-276). San Francisco: Jossey-Bass.

Nachmann, B. (1960). Childhood experience and vocational choice in law, dentistry, and social work. *Journal of Counseling Psychology, 7,* 243-250.

O'Brien, K., Friedman, S. C., Tipton, L. C., & Linn, S. G. (2000). Attachment, separation, and women's vocational development: A longitudinal analysis. *Journal of Counseling Psychology, 47,* 301-315.

O'Donnell, D. A., & Anderson, D. G. (1978). Factors influencing choice of major and career of capable women. *Vocational Guidance Quarterly, 26,* 214-221.

Penick, N. I., & Jepsen, D. A. (1992). Family functioning and adolescent career development. *Career Development Quarterly, 40,* 208-222.

Peterson, G. W., Stivers, M. E., & Peters, D. F. (1986). Family versus nonfamily significant others for the career decisions of low-income youth. *Family Relations: Journal of Applied Family and Child Studies, 35*(3), 417-424.

Rainey, L. M., & Borders, L. D. (1997). Influential factors in career orientation and career aspiration of early adolescent girls. *Journal of Counseling Psychology, 44*(2), 160-172.

Rosen, D., Holmberg, K., & Holland, J. L. (1994). *Self-directed search: The educational opportunities finder.* Odessa, FL: Psychological Assessment Resources.

Standley, K., & Soule, B. (1974). Women in male-dominated professions: Contrasts in their personal and vocational histories. *Journal of Vocational Behavior, 4,* 245-258.

Switzer, D. K., Grigg, A. E., Miller, J. S., & Young, R. K. (1962). Early experiences and occupational choice: A test of Roe's hypothesis. *Journal of Counseling Psychology, 9,* 45-48.

Tangri, S. S. (1972). Determinants of occupational role innovation among college women. *Journal of Social Issues, 28,* 177-199.

Thornton, A., & Freedman, D. (1998). *Intergenerational study of parents and children, 1962-1993.* (Computer file, 2nd ICPSR version). Ann Arbor, MI: University of Michigan,

Trice, A. D. (1991). A retrospective study of career development: Relationship among first aspirations, parental occupations, and current occupations. *Psychological Reports, 68,* 287-290.

Trigg, L. J., & Perlman, D. (1976). Social influences on women's pursuit of a nontraditional career. *Psychology of Women Quarterly, 1,* 138-150.

Vondracek, F. W., Lerner, R. M., & Schulenberg, J. E. (1986). *Career development: A life-span developmental approach.* Hillsdale, NJ: Erlbaum.

Weishaar, M., Green, B., & Craighead, L. (1981). Primary influences of initial vocational choices for college women. *Journal of Vocational Behavior, 18,* 67-78.

Whiston, S. C., & Keller, B. K. (2004). The influences of the family of origin on career development: A review and analysis. *The Counseling Psychologist, 32,* 493-568.

Zingaro, J. C. (1983). A family systems approach for the career counselor. *Personnel and Guidance Journal, 62,* 24-27.

ABOUT THE AUTHORS

Donald W. Anderson Sr. is an associate professor in the Department of Behavioral Studies and Educational Leadership in the College of Education at Southern University and A&M College in Baton Rouge, LA. He held various positions with the public school system in Baton Rouge, LA. before retiring after 25 years. He currently teaches a variety of graduate level counseling courses that include: Social and Cultural Foundations in Counseling, Theories of Vocational Development, Multicultural Counseling, Behavioral Science and the Law (Ethics), Group Dynamics, Personality and Developmental Dynamics, Practicum, and Internship in Professional Counseling. He is a nationally certified counselor (NCC) and a licensed professional counselor (LPC). He holds membership in The American Psychological Association (APA), the Louisiana Counseling Association (LCA), Chi Sigma Iota, Phi Delta Kappa, and the Louisiana Vocational Association (LVA). Dr. Anderson is on the editorial board of the National Association of Student Affairs Professional Journal. He also serves on the Region 6 Head Start Review Team and is the mental health consultant for the East Baton Rouge Parish Head Start Program. He has provided mental health consultations and made presentations at workshops and conferences in various parts of the country on topics such as child abuse, emotional development of children, substance abuse, family therapy, grief counseling and therapy, mental health issues in children and adolescents, at-risk populations, multicultural counseling, and vocational counseling and assessment.

Nancy L. Crumpton is currently associate professor and chair of the Counseling Department at Troy University Montgomery Campus, Montgomery, AL. She is a licensed professional counselor (LPC), licensed supervising counselor, certified case manager, senior disability analyst and psychometrist. Her work experiences have included positions at a comprehensive rehabilitation facility, community mental health center, as a counselor in a nontraditional high school, and rehabilitation consultant with substance abuse treatment programs, insurance companies, Social Security Administration, Department of Labor (O.W.C.P.) and forensic cases. In addition to her work at Troy University she has a part-time private practice working with individuals who are interested in changing careers or career direction (college students) and with persons with disabilities that are required to change careers due to functional limitations. Her research is focused on developing a counseling model that incorporates detailed use of occupational information, determination of transferable skills and local labor market data to assist in career decision-making, development of self assessment skills and teaching optimism when working with college students and persons with disabilities. She is also participating in the development of a supervising counselor online training program.

Grafton T. Eliason is currently assistant professor and coordinator of the School Counseling Program, Department of Counselor Education and Services, California University of Pennsylvania. Dr. Eliason has taught courses in career counseling and has a special interest in career development in our schools. He received his doctorate in counselor education and supervision from Duquesne University (CACREP). He has also earned a MEd. in school counseling from Shippensburg University (CACREP) and a MDiv. from Princeton Theological Seminary. He has numerous certifications including certified school counselor (K-12) in Pennsylvania, licensed professional counselor (LPC) in Pennsylvania, and national certified counselor (NCC). He has also taught at the Citadel, Duquesne University, and Chatham College. Past positions in counseling include serving as an elementary school counselor for Northern York School District and working as a therapist in private practice at Pathways Counseling Services in Pennsylvania. Dr. Eliason has published and presented on existential theory, person centered theory, solution focused theory, death anxiety, grief, and loss. He can be contacted at graftoneliason@hotmail.com.

Joseph M. Garmon is a graduate of the Combined Doctoral Program in Counseling Psychology and School Psychology, Florida State University. He is now in Private practice in Thomasville, Georgia. His research interests include career development and career assessment.

Jessica Grasha recently graduated from California University of Pennsylvania with a master's of education degree in elementary guidance. Her research interests include career development interventions within elementary, intermediate, and middle school settings.

Briana K. Keller recently completed her doctorate in counseling psychology at Indiana University. She is now working as a career counselor in the Center for Career Services at the University of Washington. She also works as an adjunct professor in the Counseling & School Psychology department at Seattle University, where she teaches lifespan career development. Her primary research interest is the relationship between the family of origin and career development across the lifespan.

John D. Krumboltz is a professor in the School of Education, Stanford University and is a fellow of the American Psychological Association and the American Association for the Advancement of Science. He is also the recipient of the Leona Tyler Award, Division of Counseling Psychology. His research interests include career development, career counseling, career assessment, and multicultural factors in career choice.

Amy Lucas recently graduated from California University of Pennsylvania with a master's of education degree in secondary guidance. Her research interests include career development and career counseling with adolescents and young adults.

Spencer G. Niles is a professor and department head for Counselor Education, Counseling Psychology, and Rehabilitation Services at the Pennsylvania State University. He has also served as president of the National Career Development Association (2003-2004), president of the Pennsylvania Association of Counselor Education and Supervision (2001-2002), president of the Virginia Career Development Association (1993–1995) and as editor of *The Career Development Quarterly* (1998-2003). His awards include the American Counseling Association Extended Research Award (2004), Fellow of the National Career Development Association, American Counseling Association David Brooks Distinguished Mentor Award (2003), Honorary Member, Japanese Career Development Association (2003), Lifetime Honorary Membership, Ohio Career Development Association (2003), and University of British Columbia Noted Scholar Award (2001). He has been a visiting scholar at several international universities, author or coauthor of over 80 publications, delivered over 89 presentations at international, national, and regional conferences, served in a variety of administrative and leadership positions, current member of five editorial boards, and has noted grant writing experience.

John Patrick is an associate professor and outcomes assessment coordinator, Department of Counselor Education and Services, California University of Pennsylvania. He has taught numerous courses in career counseling and has a special interest in career counseling with persons with psychiatric disabilities. He has published on various career topics including career assessment, curriculum development, and vocational rehabilitation. He has been a reviewer for several state and national journals. Dr. Patrick is a certified rehabilitation counselor (CRC), national certified counselor (NCC), and licensed professional counselor (LPC) in Pennsylvania. He has also taught at The Pennsylvania State University, Minnesota State University-Moorhead, and Troy University Montgomery Campus. Past positions include serving as a vocational rehabilitation counselor, Job Corps counselor and counseling director, and various career and academic advising positions in higher education. He has held various leadership positions with the American College Counseling Association, Pennsylvania Association of Counselor Education and Supervision, Alabama Association of Counselor Education and Supervision, and the Greater Pittsburgh Counseling Association and is active with the American Educational Research Association and the American Counseling Association. He can be reached at patrick@cup.edu.

April Perry recently graduated from California University of Pennsylvania with a master's of education degree in elementary guidance. She currently resides in Little Egg Harbor, New Jersey. Her research interest is in incorporating a holistic approach to career development programming with elementary school classes.

Gary W. Peterson is a professor and program coordinator of Psychological Services in Education, Department of Educational Psychology and Learning Systems, Florida State University. He is also the clinical training director of the Combined Doctoral Program in Counseling Psychology and School Psychology. He is a licensed psychologist in Florida. His research interests include career problem solving and decision making, personality measurement and assessment, and educational evaluation and accountability.

Erik J. Porfeli is an assistant professor at the University of North Carolina at Charlotte. He earned a doctorate in human development and family studies from Pennsylvania State University and masters of education degree in rehabilitation counseling from Kent State University. Prior to graduate study, he earned a bachelor of science degree in psychology from the University of Pittsburgh and was employed as a social worker for over 5 years. Over the past several years, Porfeli has collaborated with others to publish empirical and theoretical work devoted to vocational development across the childhood, adolescent, and young adult periods employing developmental contextual and developmental systems perspectives. His dissertation employed both perspectives to study and test the dynamic link between work values and work experiences with longitudinal data spanning the high school years. Porfeli has served on the editorial board of the *Career Development Quarterly* for the past 2 years. In his present position at UNC-Charlotte, he teaches research methods and statistic courses to graduate students in the College of Education.

Donald L. Thompson was professor of higher education and counseling psychology at the University of Connecticut from 1971 to 1995. From 1995 to 2002, he was dean of the College of Education at Troy State University Montgomery. He was one of the two original founders of the Career Development Special Interest Group of the American Educational Research Association. He is now a licensed psychologist in private practice in Chandler Arizona.

Kelly Tuning is currently working in the Crisis Unit of Mercy Behavioral Health, Pittsburgh, Pennsylvania as supervisor of the adult diversion and acute stabilization program. She received her master's of science degree in community/agency counseling from California University of Pennsylvania. She is a member of the Pittsburgh Critical Incident Stress Management (CISM) team, which conducts debriefings and provides on scene support to help those involved in rescue and recovery. She can be contacted at KTuning@mercybh.org.

Jerry Trusty is a professor in the Department of Counselor Education, Counseling Psychology and Rehabilitation Services at The Pennsylvania State University. He is coordinator of the secondary school counseling program. Dr. Trusty has worked as a middle-school and high-school counselor, a school-dropout prevention coordinator, and as a counselor educator. His research and scholarly work has focused on school dropout prevention, adolescent educational and career development, parental influences on adolescents, multicultural counseling, and family influences on counselor-trainees.

Susan C. Whiston is a professor in the Department of Counseling and Educational Psychology at Indiana University. She received her PhD from the University of Wyoming in 1986. Her current research interests are in the areas of career counseling and school counseling, with a focus on outcome research. Dr. Whiston is the author of *Principles and Applications of Assessment in Counseling* and a number of book chapters and articles. In addition, she currently serves on the editorial board for the *Journal of Career Assessment* and the *Career Development Quarterly*.

Lightning Source UK Ltd.
Milton Keynes UK
UKOW06f0754131116
287460UK00012B/458/P